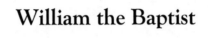

William the Baptist

William the Baptist

by James M. Chaney

(Updated and annotated by J. Ed Eubanks, Jr.)

The idea of writing "William the Baptist" in the form here presented, was suggested while endeavoring to draw from a class in Sabbath-school the meaning of Paul in Romans 6:3-4. My work was to frame and propound questions, by means of which a clear view of the passage is obtained.

To that class in the Sabbath-school of the Presbyterian Church of Lexington, Missouri, of which—

Miss BESSIE GATTRELL, Lee's Summit, MO.,

Miss MATTIE WEIDEMEYER, Clinton, MO.,

Miss FANNIE HOSS, Sedalia, MO.,

Miss AMANDA TRIMBLE, Plattsburg, MO.,

Miss ANNA AYLSWORTH, Clarinda, Iowa,

were members, while attending as pupils "The Elizabeth Aull Female Seminary," of which was president, this little volume is respectfully dedicated by the author.

FROM THE EDITOR:

While I was in college, I appealed to my pastor to help me understand the validity of my own infant baptism, performed by "sprinkling." He said to me frankly, "You and I could dialogue about it for hours, but it might be faster if you simply took this book home and read it, then returned with any questions." Then he handed me a copy of *William the Baptist*. As I left his office, my pastor said, "Keep it until you finish it, but I must get that copy back — it is my only copy, and the book is out-of-print."

I quickly realized the value of the book he had lent me, and having become convinced by its contents, I began to seek a copy of my own. Over the years, I have accumulated copies, lent out my own, and always longed for a new, updated version that was readily and affordably available. I am delighted to work with Doulos Resources to produce just such a version.

It has been my aim from the start to stay out of the way of Chaney's excellent thinking, writing, and theology. He does not need me to provide a better or more complete version of what he has produced; on its own, the book has done just fine. My goal, instead, is to update those few words that have changed in spelling, usage, or style to its contemporary counterpart, to impose formatting that allows a more pleasing presentation than the facsimile editions that seem to be available today, and to offer comments, definitions, or explanation in footnote where useful. I have amended the Scripture references, removing the Roman numerals and replacing them with modern citation styles, and I have replaced the King James language with that of the English Standard Version when Chaney included portions of the text itself. You will note that, occasionally, I have also offered a Scripture reference in footnote; for whatever reason, Chaney did not elect to include the reference in the original (probably because, unlike our more biblically-illiterate culture, those in Chaney's day would have known the verses without need of reference). Finally, I have provided a Scripture Index, which serves as both a useful reference tool as well as a testimony to the extent to which *William the Baptist* is grounded in Scripture.

I pray that you will find my editing and annotations to be a help, and not a hindrance, to allowing Chaney's fine book to minister to yet another generation.

TABLE OF CONTENTS

GENERAL REMARKS

The Bible is the best work on the subject of baptism. In the early part of my ministry, when the Presbytery was in session at the church of which I had just taken charge, a colporteur[1] in attendance introduced me to a gentleman who, as he thought, ought to unite with the church. After a short conversation with him, I agreed with the colporteur, and remarked that the Session would meet in a few minutes, and suggested that he should present himself for admission into the church. After a moment's pause, he said he was "laboring under a difficulty that rendered such a step impracticable."

Upon inquiry I found that he believed that immersion is the proper mode of baptism. I told him that was no difficulty; in D— was a Baptist church, where he would be welcomed.

"But," said he, "I prefer the Presbyterian Church."

---

[1] The French adaptation of the middle-French word *comporteur*, itself an adaptation of the English *comporter*— a peddler of religious books.

1

The colporteur proposed to sell him some books on the subject of baptism. My reply was, "Mr. E., let his books alone. If you have immersion in your head, my first advice to you is, go and unite with the Baptist Church. If you are not satisfied, take your Bible alone, and examine the subject in the light of God's Word, praying for the guidance of the Spirit; after such examination, act according to the conclusion reached."

About four months after this conversation, he presented himself to the Session of our church for admission. I asked him if he was satisfied on the question of baptism. His answer was, "thoroughly."

He proved to be one of the most intelligent Bible Christians I ever knew, and remarkable for the conscientious discharge of duty. As I subsequently learned, every influence had been exerted on him to convince him that immersion is baptism.

What the people want is not a learned dissertation on the classic meaning of words in a language of which they know nothing, but a simple exposition of passages in the Bible with which they are familiar.

In the following treatise I have confined myself to the Word of God alone, examining the subject in what I conceive to be an exhaustive method, namely:

1. To ascertain the meaning of the word used to designate the rite; to do this by examining those passages where the word occurs, and, from the context and attending circumstances, to ascertain in what sense the word is used by the sacred writers.

2. To inquire what is the significance of the rite, and see what light this throws on the question of mode.

3. To examine the cases of its administration found recorded in the New Testament; to examine these in the light of circumstantial evidence.

2

These methods are independent of each other; and if they unite in bringing us to the same conclusion, we may be assured that we have the truth.

I have chosen the conversational method of discussion, because it serves better than any other to bring to the attention of the reader the particular point to be impressed on the mind. The only objection to such a method is that it offers temptations to caricature the views we would assail. I have endeavored carefully to avoid such a weakness.

It was not my purpose to introduce anything of the romantic; but this seemed the only practicable method of introducing the discussion, and bringing out certain points regarded of great importance: from the place assigned it by Jesus, as a symbol of the Spirit's work, down to the useless purpose of symbolizing, in a very awkward manner, an event that had nothing to do with man's redemption.

The evil of such perversion is aggravated when we remember it necessitates the denial, on the part of immersionists, that we form any part of the church of God .

If we are in error, let us acknowledge it, and have our practice correspond with the truth. If our practice is in accordance with the command of the Savior, let us not hesitate to affirm that immersion is not a scriptural mode of baptism.

Some will object to such a view as extreme, and think it as objectionable as the claims of immersionists on the question of mode. The view of some is that one mode is as good as another, and that it is a question not worthy of discussion. But such must remember what is involved in this statement. It implies that the significance of the rite is of no importance, because the whole difference centers here. Transubstantiation is no greater perversion of the Lord's Supper than is the burial theory a perversion of baptism. When immersionists abandon this theory, they will not be slow in conforming their mode to the simplicity of the gospel.

If any apology is needed for presenting this discussion to the public, I am happy to be able to lay a share of the responsibility on many friends who read the manuscript and urged its publication, and especially among these, the Rev. Drs. J. L. Yantis, John Montgomery, and N. L. Rice, who, having carefully read the manuscript, encouraged me to hope that its publication might be attended with profit to the church of God. With the prayer that God will bless it in checking, in some measure, the gross perversion of a sacred rite, I bid it go wherever readers may be found.

WILLIAM THE BAPTIST

On a bright summer evening, about the middle of June, as I was sitting with my wife in the front yard of the parsonage, Mr. William Meadows, a promising young lawyer, passed very leisurely, as if enjoying an evening walk. As he reached the gate, I thought I noticed an indication of a half-formed resolution to stop; but politely bowing, he passed on. In a few minutes he returned, and at the gate the same motions were repeated. About fifteen minutes later, we saw him again returning with a firm step and somewhat accelerated speed. But his speed slackened as he approached us, and after a hasty glance he turned his face towards the opposite side of the street, and seeing his friend K. seated in his front yard, quietly reading a newspaper, he leisurely crossed over, and standing at the gate entered into a friendly chat with him. His movements had already attracted my attention, and somewhat excited my curiosity, and I determined to watch and wait. I noticed that he frequently cast a look over his shoulder towards us. It was, perhaps, ten minutes after he had taken his position at the gate, that my wife was called to attend to some domestic duty. No sooner was her absence noted than he bade his friend good evening, and hastened across the street to where I was sitting. The cause of his movements was soon explained. In one week from that evening, he desired my presence at the house of one of my members, to unite his fortunes with those of Miss Dora G, a young lady of rare excellence and cultivation, and one of the most active and efficient members of my charge.

I cannot say that I was surprised, for such a thing had been whispered as a probability. I cannot say that I was pleased or displeased at the announcement. This undecided state of mind did not arise from any indifference to my young friend, Dora. Mr. M was a young man, about four and twenty, of excellent family; of decided mental endowments, had graduated with the highest honors at one of the best colleges in the land; had attended a law school, and was now well established in his profession.

But Dora was a Presbyterian; one of my most useful members abounding in every good work. Mr. M, though not a member of the church, yet was in principle a most zealous Baptist, evangelistic in his disposition, always ready to contend for the peculiarities of this church, even to a disagreeable degree. This peculiarity in his disposition had been developed at an early period, when he was a youth of fourteen or fifteen. The occasion of it, or the time when it first expressed itself, was a public discussion on the question of baptism, in which he took a deep interest. The whole community had become interested; discussion was rife, and no one was a more active disputant than the youthful William. When the discussion had been dropped by others, and the subject had lost most of its interest to them, the zeal of young William seemed to grow stronger. His zeal gave him such prominence as a defender of Baptist peculiarities, that, by common consent, he was known as "William the Baptist. The nickname was not displeasing to him. He regarded it as a reward for his youthful zeal. He may have become weary of the title, but it followed him to college, and so universal was its use that grave professors, in speaking of him, designated him as William the

Baptist. It clung to him in the law school, and as the promising practitioner, it was "William the Baptist."

At the appointed time, a pleasant company was assembled at the house of Mr. G, and our young friends, William and Dora, were duly united as husband and wife according to the ordinance of God.

As I left the happy company, I wondered what manner of life awaited them; she an intelligent, devoted Presbyterian; he, though not a member, yet, in principle, an over-zealous Baptist. I remembered the question of old, "Do two walk together unless they have agreed to meet?"[1]

There was, to human view, no hope that he would ever unite with the Presbyterian Church, and I supposed there was as little probability that she would ever consent to become a Baptist.

It would seem that Dora guessed my state of mind, and, knowing the interest I had always felt in her welfare, about two weeks after marriage she called at the parsonage, and in a short time introduced the subject herself, when the following conversation was held:

DORA.— "I am sure you are curious to know how such people, so different in their religious views, and so set in them, expect to get along as husband and wife."

PASTOR.— "I confess it has been a matter of great concern to me. But there is no impossibility in your living together in peace, if you both can agree to disagree."

D.— "And that we have agreed to do. We talked that matter over, and came to a definite understanding before our marriage. We agreed not to discuss our differences."

P.— "Domestic peace is assured so long as this covenant between you is kept. But the bond of love, uniting husband and wife, will

---

[1] Amos 3:3

7

prove but a rotten hempen cord to the bitter jealousies engendered by religious controversy."

D.– "I never did discuss such matters with anyone, and I have no desire to discuss them with William; for apart from the evil consequences of which you speak, I know I could effect nothing with him."

I invoked the blessing of God on them, and earnestly implored him that they might live long and happily together, and thus our interview on this subject ended. They lived in a house not far from the parsonage, and we saw Dora almost every day. She was, as before, a regular attendant at church, at the morning and evening service. William usually accompanied her, especially at the evening service. Thus the weeks and months passed on, and no couple in S. were happier than they.

The pastor of the Baptist church was an excellent man, unusually liberal in his views, and seemed to sympathize with Paul in his statement, "Christ did not send me to baptize, but to preach the gospel."[2] His church was in a flourishing condition. He was loved and respected by all. He was always ready to unite with all in every good work.

But he soon found himself beset with difficulties. A member of his church, who had married a young lady in connection with the Methodist church, during a protracted meeting in the latter church, had, on a communion Sunday, celebrated the Lord's Supper with his wife. At a church meeting of the Baptists, the matter was brought up for the purpose of disciplining the young man for his departure from the faith.

Some of the members were free in their use of harsh language in condemnation of the offense. They thought there was a limit to Christian charity, and that limit had been passed in the present instance, and in other cases that might be mentioned, and their

---

[2] 1 Corinthians 1:17

only hope to put an end to such departures was to deal briefly with the offenders. The pastor listened to the discussion for some time, and perceiving that the zeal of some was not according to knowledge, ventured to quote to them the language of Paul: "Brothers, if anyone is caught in any transgression, you who are spiritual should restore him in a spirit of gentleness. Keep watch on yourself, lest you too be tempted."[3] As the offender was absent, he suggested the propriety of appointing a committee of prudent brothers, who should wait on him, and hear what he had to say in extenuation of his offense, and for the committee to report at the next church meeting. Scarcely was the pastor seated when it became evident that a storm was approaching. One, hastily arising, repeated, in a derisive tone, the language of the pastor, "to see what he has to say in extenuation of his offense," and continued, "if that is to be the object of the committee, we need wait no longer." The pastor soon learned that the "other instances" in which the bounds of charity had been passed referred to his fellowshiping with other denominations. It was the pastor's turn now to become excited; at least, he felt it to be his duty to administer a merited rebuke to some of the brothers for their excess of zeal.

This led to recrimination, and it soon became apparent that the great transgressor, in the eyes of some, was the pastor himself. Some of the more zealous were inclined to excuse the offense of the young brother, affirming that he had been led into the commission of the offense by the example of the pastor. Thus, affairs took an unexpected turn. The result of that church meeting was, the pastor soon had to seek a new field of labor.

About a year after the marriage of William and Dora, a new pastor filled the pulpit of the Baptist Church. He was a man of learning, of pulpit ability, ultra in his views, and evangelizing in his disposition. He was a frequent visitor at the house of William. It was not long until Dora was frequently seen alone at the Sabbath night

---

[3] Galatians 6:1

service. The new pastor was exerting a decided influence on William; and Dora, though compelled to go to her own church alone, consoled herself with the hope that her husband might be led to make a public confession of his faith in Christ. She did not indulge a hope that he would ever become a Presbyterian, and her first desire was that he might become a Christian, and would greatly prefer that he should be a member of the Baptist Church to his having no connection with any.

In making a short call one evening and finding William absent, the new pastor, as he was about to leave, made some remark about religious differences between husbands and wives, and, in a joking manner, asked her if she could not make a good Presbyterian out of William.

Her reply, in the same tone, was, "What! William the Baptist? No indeed; I would as soon undertake to make a Presbyterian out of you."

This seemed to please him, and after speaking a few words in commendation of her husband's intelligence, and the importance of his making a public-profession of his faith, as he gave evidence, he thought, of being a converted man, he took his departure.

On the next Sunday night, William asked his wife if she would like to accompany him to the Baptist Church.

She readily consented to do so. The sermon was on the text, "But Caleb followed the Lord fully."[4] The discourse was an able one, in which the preacher showed what it is to follow the Lord fully, drawing a beautiful picture of a man or woman devoted, soul and body, to the Lord and his service. At the close, in a very ingenious manner, he drew a picture of Christ descending into the Jordan, and there, by the hands of John, "to fulfill all righteousness," was buried beneath the wave. He said there were many who desired to follow Christ, and did follow him in what they conceived to be the

---

[4] This is a fragment of Numbers 14:24.

10

spirit of his commandments, but who did not think it necessary to follow him "beneath the wave." They followed him, but not like Caleb, fully. Such persons, he said, should remember the words of the Savior as he was about to enter the watery grave, "Thus it is fitting for us to *fulfill all righteousness.*"[5]

He assumed that all acknowledged that Jesus "entered the watery grave," but that some persuaded themselves that it was not essential to follow him there; they thought that some other mode of baptism would answer the purpose; and again reminded them that Caleb was commended because he followed the Lord fully; and Jesus himself was immersed in the Jordan to fulfill all righteousness.

After the benediction was pronounced, there was a rush of the sisters to express their kindly feeling for William and his wife. Her little arms fairly ached from the numerous hand-shakings.

The pastor, with a humble smile, greeted them, and jokingly said to her, "Remember what I said to you about this husband of yours. Do not despair; give it a try, and you may succeed."

But to this Dora made no response. The very thought of their opening a discussion of their differences in religious matters filled her with horror. She had no desire to attempt to make a Presbyterian of her husband, and had just as little desire that any such attempt should be made to effect a change in her views.

Early in the fall, there was a festival for the purpose of raising money to re-furnish the Baptist church. William intimated that it would please him if Dora would render some assistance, which she cheerfully consented to do. As was her custom in all good works, she entered into it with all her soul, expressing as much interest in its success as if it had been for the benefit of her own church. Some of the Baptist friends misinterpreted her zeal. Her activity at the festival, and her frequent attendance at the Baptist church with

---

[5] Matthew 3:15.

William, afforded an occasion for the rumor that she would soon join them, with her husband.

Her pastor heard of the rumor, but felt sure that it was without foundation.

One circumstance, however, seemed unaccountable to him, and that was, she had never shown any concern about the baptism of her child, now about six months old. He was unwilling to make any allusion to the matter, as he thought it probable her husband would be decided in his opposition to her presenting her child for baptism; but he expected that she would, at least, speak of it, and express her sorrow that circumstances were such as to render it impossible for her to discharge that pleasing duty.

Not long after such thoughts had filled her pastor's mind, Dora presented herself at the parsonage, obviously under some excitement. The occasion of her excitement was soon explained. She had spoken to her husband about the baptism of her child, and the mere suggestion of the question seemed greatly to annoy him. He expressed his contempt for that "relic of popery, baby sprinkling." The feelings of Dora were wounded as they had never been before by him.

She was silent— was sorry that she had referred to the matter.

He soon saw that he had, without any reason, spoken harshly, and after some time of mutual silence he told her he had no objection to her having the child baptized, as he knew it would gratify her, and could do the child no harm.

But she determined to say nothing more about it. It was not long, however, before he again referred to it, and urged her to do it if it would gratify her. And now she wanted advice; what should she do under the circumstances?

Her pastor told her that if she thought her husband was sincere in urging her to present the child, though his motive was only to gratify her, as he expressed it, yet he thought she should do so. As a result of this interview, the mother, on the next Saturday, presented her child, and in the solemn ordinance of baptism, dedicated it to God. It was a solemn service. As the mother took upon herself the vows to bring up the child for Jesus, to whom it was consecrated, she wept, and many, knowing her peculiar circumstances, wept with her; and from many a heart there went up a silent "amen," as the pastor implored the covenant-keeping God for blessings on the mother and child.

Not long after this, the Baptist minister, in one of his visits, took occasion again to ask her about her success with her husband in "making a good Presbyterian of him." She told him the subject had never been mentioned by either of them, and could not be without the violation of a solemn pledge they had mutually made to each other before marriage.

He said he sympathized with her, and agreed with her that it was a very delicate subject. But he feared these differences in their religious views resulted in evil to her husband, keeping him out of the church, as he was unwilling to be in connection with one church and his wife in another. This touched a tender chord in Dora, and its vibrations were evident. She believed her husband to be a Christian, and had long wished that he would unite with the people of his choice, as she had no hope that he could ever be anything but a Baptist.

To this the minister replied that such separation between husband and wife was, on many accounts, a very unpleasant state of things. He had no disposition to press for conversion; that, he thought, was a most contemptible work; and rather than William should longer continue out of the church, he would use his influence to have him unite with her.

Dora was pleased with the unselfish interest demonstrated for her husband's spiritual welfare. She thanked him, but told him that, however painful it would be for them thus to be separated, yet there was no help for it, and she hoped William would, without delay, make public profession of his faith in Christ, and unite with the Baptist Church.

He then suggested that there could be no harm in talking the matter over with him, to see if they could not make some compromise, and if she would give her consent, he would talk the matter over with her husband, and urge him to go with her. She again expressed her gratitude for his kindness, and agreed with him that no harm could result from the attempt. It was agreed that he should present the matter to William, and if circumstances were favorable, all should, at an early period, talk the subject over together.

A few days after this, Dora was greatly surprised to hear William introduce the subject as they were seated quietly in their room after Supper. He told her that it had been his wish— as he had felt it to be his duty— to be numbered with the people of God, but was greatly troubled by the differences in their religious views, and until now he could not mention his trouble because of the pledge they had made; but now, as he supposed, they were both released from that agreement. He expressed a willingness to make almost any sacrifice to have the differences removed, but thought it would require less sacrifice on her part to go with him to the Baptist Church, than for him to go with her.

Dora in this language saw fresh troubles. She saw that the way had been opened for profitless controversy. She did not wish to discuss the question in any such form. She could not be received into the Baptist church without repudiating her baptism, and this she could not and would not do. But she did not desire to argue the matter, and heartily wished she had not given her consent to have the subject mentioned to William. But what could she do? She must make some reply. After a moment's pause, she told him she thought they had better not discuss the subject, but to do as they had agreed before marriage, "agree to disagree," and urged him to discharge his duty, and apply at once for admission into the Baptist Church.

William was not prepared for such a response. He wanted to talk the matter over with her; he felt sure that he could convince her that he was right, and that she ought to go with him to the Baptist Church.

As she displayed such a decided aversion to discuss the subject, though disappointed, he dropped it. But he could not dismiss it from his mind. He felt sure that, if he could gain her consent to go over the whole subject of baptism with him, she would see and acknowledge her error, and readily go with him.

His difficulties seemed to increase. He had hoped; now he despaired. After striving for some time to dismiss the subject from his thoughts and failing, he arose, put on his hat, and leisurely walked out. But no sooner had he reached the pavement than his speed was accelerated, and in a few minutes he found himself at the house of Rev. Mr. R., the Baptist minister. To him he told his troubles; said his condition was like that of the Israelites in Egypt after they had mentioned their troubles in hope of getting some relief. Afterwards it was worse with them than before. He then told of his interview with his wife, and the result of it; "and now," said he, "what am I to do?"

Mr. R.– "Do not despair; let patience have her perfect work. Did you tell her that you would, on any conditions, unite with her?"

W.– "No, I did not. I would not except on an impossible condition, and that is that they would immerse me. I know they would not receive me on such a condition."

Mr. R.– "But I have known Presbyterian ministers who would immerse, rather than fail to secure a desirable member."

W.– "But Mr. C. will not."

Mr. R.– "His refusal may have a good effect on Dora. It will enable her to see how unreasonable it is; to see that the compromise must be all on one side. It could not fail, I am sure, to have a good effect her; better than any argument you can advance.

15

Besides, it is an argument to which she will be compelled to listen."

William was again encouraged. He felt sure that he would be safe in offering to unite with the church of his wife on the condition named; and being refused, he felt sure, as Mr. R. suggested, that it would prove a powerful argument to induce his wife to go with him.

He was soon again seated by her side, with hope stronger than ever that his troubles would soon be over, and that Dora would be with him in the church of his choice.

After some general conversation carried on in a pleasant tone, fixing his eyes on her, and smiling, he said, "Dora, I have some good news for you. As it seems impossible for you to become a Baptist, I have made up my mind to apply for membership in your church."

Dora was startled. She was not prepared for such an announcement. She knew not what to think, nor how to reply.

At last she said, "I am afraid, my dear husband, you have reached this conclusion without mature deliberation."

It was his turn to be surprised. He had expected that his announcement would be received with joy, and that she would encourage him to carry out his resolution. But her remark was calculated to cause him to hesitate, to reconsider and to change his purpose. After a little pause, recovering from the astonishment her remark had produced, he said: "wife, I do not understand you, you will have to explain your meaning."

"I mean," said she, "that in religion we should be governed entirely by our convictions of duty, and not by a desire to please any mortal, though it be father or mother, husband or wife. Do you not remember the language of Paul, 'for am I now seeking the approval of man, or of God? Or am I trying to please man? If I were still trying to please man, I would not be a servant of Christ.'[6] In

---

[6] Galatians 1:10.

religion, however painful it may be, yet if necessary, we must forsake father and mother, husband and wife."

Every word she spoke served to increase his astonishment. After her last utterances, his hope was not as bright as when he had, a short time before, reached his home, and taken his seat by her side.

But she must, he thought, hear my proposal. "I have," he said, "carefully considered the matter. As I told you, I am ready to make almost any sacrifice that I may be with my wife in the church. As you well know, my decided preference is for the Baptist Church. But I can, with a good conscience, live in the Presbyterian Church. They do not require their members to subscribe to all their doctrines, as I heard your pastor say from his pulpit not long ago."

DORA.— "But, my dear husband, how about your reception— your baptism?"

W.— "That is the only difficulty; but that is a very small one. As I am willing to go more than half way in the compromise, your pastor would not be so exacting and unreasonable as to refuse to favor me in that small particular. I have known Presbyterian ministers that would immerse."

Dora saw no solution of their troubles. She felt very sure that her pastor would not favor him in that particular.

From her own brief examination of the subject, she had reached the conclusion that it is very questionable whether a Presbyterian minister can, with consistency, administer that sacred rite by immersion.

These views she kept to herself, as she wished to avoid discussion; but she told her husband that in all probability he would meet with disappointment, if he expected Mr. C. would immerse him.

But William insisted that they should call on Mr. C., make a plain statement of all their difficulties, and that he would make application for membership, and see what the result would be.

With reluctance Dora consented: she not only felt that it would result in no good, but greatly feared that it might make matters worse; for she felt certain her pastor would refuse to immerse her husband, and such refusal would serve to render him more determined in his opposition to her church.

On the following Monday evening, the proposed visit was made. They found Mr. C. in a happy mood, and, from appearances, it was evident that he had been romping, in what some might regard a rather unclerical manner, with his children. Almost immediately after they were seated, a little three-year-old, with handkerchief in hand, approached him and said, longingly, "Now, pa, you be blindfolded *adain*, and let us hide. I know you *tant* find me, for ma said she would put me in de *tubboard*."

The little ones looked disappointed at their coming, as it seemed to put an end to their evening sport. Mr. C. said Monday was his rest day, and very frequently on Monday night he gave himself up to the children, to be as one of them in all their childish amusements. William and Dora began to think that they were intruding, but were soon made to feel perfectly at ease, as provision was made in an adjoining room for the children to amuse themselves; and judging from their childish laughter, they soon forgot that strangers had broken into their arrangements for their evening sports.

William's mind was too full of the business for which the visit had been made to allow a long delay in introducing it.

But just how to begin he did not know. On the day preceding, there had been five or six additions to the Presbyterian Church, and William took occasion to say that it seemed there was some interest on the subject of religion in Mr. C.'s congregation.

To this Mr. C. replied, and gave some account of the interest expressed, and expressed a hope that there would be a general awakening. And, greatly to the relief of William, addressing him personally, he said: "I have been wondering for some time why you do not take in hand the all-important question of your soul's eternal interest."

W.— "That subject has occupied my attention for a long time. For some months past especially, it has been the occasion of no little trouble to me."

PASTOR.— "The matter is very simple. Your condition as a sinner is very plain, and your only hope is to accept of the Lord Jesus as your Savior."

W.— "I hope I have done so. My only hope is in his righteousness; and this is my only plea."

P.— "Then you are a Christian; for 'we are all the children of God by faith in Christ Jesus,'[7] and pleading the righteousness of Jesus is the faith that secures our acceptance."

W.— "My present cause of trouble is in reference to my making a public profession of my faith in Jesus."

P.— "Do you not feel that it is your duty to take this step, and without delay?"

W.— "Yes, sir; I have put it off until I feel it can be postponed no longer. But what to do I know not."

P.— "Why delay?"

W.— "I am in trouble on the question of baptism. My views on this subject are very decided. I feel that it is my duty to follow the Savior fully, and be immersed."

P.— "And what is to hinder you? I do not see how that can prove a hindrance."

---

[7] Galatians 3:26.

By this time William had become sincerely desirous of uniting with the Presbyterian Church, in order to be with his wife, if he could do it without sacrificing his convictions of duty in reference to baptism.

The last statement of the pastor was interpreted by him to indicate that his request for admission by immersion would be granted, and he felt encouraged. There was a momentary pause, after which Mr. C. continued: "I have sometimes regarded it as providential that there are different churches, as people have such different views. You will find the Baptist Church just suited to your views. And if you will permit me to give you advice, it is that you will, at the earliest opportunity, apply there for membership."

W.— "But my wife is a member of your church, and I can not bear the thought of being thus separated from her."

P.— "It is, indeed, an undesirable state of things, but it is not as bad as something worse."

W— "What could be worse?"

P.— "For your wife to be immersed against her convictions of duty; or for you to have water applied to you while believing that immersion only is baptism."

Just then the pastor's wife suggested the propriety of letting William read a small volume on the subject of baptism, and "perhaps," said she, "he may be relieved from his troubles."

But the pastor said, "No, I would not advise such a course. If he has immersion in his head as firmly as I suppose it is, my advice is, as before, go at once and seek admission into the Baptist Church. Or if your views on baptism are not entirely satisfactory; if you wish to re-examine the whole subject, take the Bible as your only book.

"Examine the subject in the light of God's word alone, asking for the guidance of His Spirit, and after such examination, act in accordance with the conclusion reached."

William listened attentively, and after a short pause, said: "I do not feel inclined to examine the subject, as my views are settled, fixed. I got them from the Word of God, and no ingenuity of man can, by any species of argument, induce me to change them."

P.— "Then your duty is plain; you are shut up to the one course."

W.— "But would you have me thus separated from my wife?"

P.— "My reply is as before. Such separation is unpleasant. But it is not as bad as something worse."

W.— "But why can we not be together?"

P.— "How can you?"

W.— "Very easily, if you will immerse me."

P.— "That I cannot do, without doing as great violence to my conscience as you would to yours in being baptized by our mode."

W.— "Then there is no help for me?"

P.— "Yes; there is one way by which your wishes can be gratified."

W.— "And what is that?"

P.— "Unite regularly with the Baptist Church; then get a certificate of membership, and apply for admission into our church."

William was thoroughly aroused on the subject of uniting with the church and being in the same church with his wife. He saw that no way was practicable, except that suggested by Mr. C., and he resolved that by this method his wishes should be gratified.

On their way home, William expressed himself as satisfied with the result of their visit, and declared his determination to unite at once with the Baptist Church, get a certificate of membership, as Mr. C. had suggested, and with that apply for membership in the Presbyterian Church.

The question that had so troubled them seemed at last solved, and the solution seemed the very best possible under the circumstances.

The next evening he visited the house of Rev. Mr. R. William felt relieved of a great burden, and the state of his mind was clearly depicted on his countenance, which had a most cheerful aspect.

Mr. R., interpreting this as favorable omen, received him with the same demonstration of cheerfulness.

W.— "I think, my dear sir, that the question which has so troubled us has, at last, found a solution."

Mr. R.— "Did Mr. C. agree to immerse you?"

W.— "No, sir; he most emphatically refused, and advised me, as my views on the subject of baptism are so fixed, to unite with the Baptist Church."

R.— "Better advice than I expected him to give. I am surprised that he did not offer you half a dozen volumes on Baptism to read, to try and convince you that Romish sprinkling is baptism."

W.— "No; his wife suggested something of the kind, but he opposed it, and said, if I was not satisfied with my views —"

R.— "To let him talk to you about it?"

W.— "No; but to go to the Bible, and to that alone."

R.— "I am as much surprised at that as at his advising you to unite with our church. He knows well enough there is no baptism in the Bible but immersion. Strange advice indeed. But Dora saw the unreasonableness of his refusing to immerse you, as I told you she would?"

W.— "No; nothing was said about that. He gave a very good reason for refusing."

R.— "And has Dora consented to unite with you?"

W.– "No, sir; I have said nothing more to her on the subject."

R.– "And yet your troubles have found a solution? I do not believe that I understand you."

W.– "It is this way. I will unite with your church, and you can give me a simple certificate of membership; this I will take to the Presbyterian Church, and be admitted on it."

R.– "Well, I must say, this is a solution! How came such a thought into your head?"

W.– "Mr. C. suggested it."

R.– "And well he might. But I am surprised that a man of your intelligence could not see the gross inconsistency of the man, in one breath refusing emphatically to immerse you, and, in the next, agreeing to take your immersion as valid baptism when administered by me. That is out-Jesuiting the Jesuits. Do you not see how grossly inconsistent it is?"

W.– "I confess I did not; but since you mention it, it does strike me as somewhat remarkable. I am sorry I did not ask him for an explanation. But if he is willing thus to receive me, the responsibility is on himself. I will go on those terms."

R.– "But, my dear sir, I hope you will excuse me from taking any part in anything so filled with trickery as that."

W.– "Will you not immerse me for that purpose?"

R.– "Emphatically, *no*. But let me tell you: you have the advantage of him; and if you will take my advice, you will follow it up. Seek an interview with him, as if you would hear his views on the subject of baptism, and take pains to fasten on him the inconsistency of which he is guilty. Take Dora with you, and let her witness his confusion, and mark my word, it will be well yet."

William was soon on his way home, thinking— "How vain are all things here below, How false, and yet how fair!"[8]

His depression was equaled only by his previous exaltation. On his reaching home, Dora at once noticed his gloomy appearance. She wondered what the cause could be, but feared to ask. He sat for some time silent, and was evidently meditating. At last he broke the silence by saying: "Well, wife, the problem I thought solved is no nearer a solution than at first."

Dora.—" My dear, what new turn have affairs taken? Has Mr. R. convinced you that you should not unite with our church?"

W.— "No; he did not attempt it."

D.— "Did he urge you to endeavor to persuade me to join his church?"

W.— "No; he said nothing about that."

D.— "What, then, is the trouble?"

W.— "He positively refuses to immerse me that I may unite with the Presbyterian Church, and I am inclined to think he is right. Do you not see how very inconsistent it is in Mr. C. to refuse to immerse me, and yet offer to take me on my immersion, if I first join the Baptist Church? I am astonished that I did not think of it when he suggested it."

D.— "My dear, it is customary for Presbyterians to receive, without re-baptism, those who apply for membership from the Baptist Church."

W.— "But think of the inconsistency of it. I will make Mr. C. feel and acknowledge its inconsistency. He will be careful hereafter never to give another such advice as he gave me."

---

[8] This is the opening line of a hymn by Isaac Watts, Book 2, hymn #48 in the collection *Hymns and Spiritual Songs by Isaac Watts* (http://www.fullbooks.com/Hymns-and-Spiritual-Songs1.html), based on Ecclesiastes 1:2.

D.— "My dear, let us drop the subject, and say nothing more about it. It has given us nothing but trouble ever since it was first mentioned. This is what I feared, and often have I been sorry that I ever gave my consent to Mr. R. to speak to you about it. Let me beg you to dismiss it from your mind; say nothing more to Mr. C., but go quietly and unite with the Baptist Church, and God will bless us both in the conscientious discharge of duty."

W.— "I confess your advice is most excellent. I now see there is no possible hope of our being together in the same church. I will take your advice in all particulars, save one. I must show Mr. C. the inconsistency of his proposal. Religion should be freed from all appearance of trickery, and I feel it to be my duty, not only to let him know that I see his inconsistency, but I intend to make him acknowledge it. I will try and get him to go over the whole question of baptism, especially in the manner he advised me to consider it— from the Bible alone. I do not think he has given much attention to the subject, and I may accomplish a good work by convincing him that I have a reason for insisting on immersion."

In a few days William met Mr. C, on the street, and told him he had changed his mind on the question of uniting with the Baptist Church in order to get a certificate to unite with the Presbyterian Church. "And with your permission," he continued, "I would like very much to have a conversation with you on the whole question of baptism. I would come to your house on any evening you could find is convenient to go over the subject with me."

Mr. C. exhibited no surprise at his change of purpose, nor did he make any inquiry as to the cause of the change.

He expressed his willingness to have a free conversation on the subject, as suggested by William, but thought one evening would not be sufficient.

He invited William to the parsonage on the Monday evening following.

FIRST EVENING: SCRIPTURE DOES NOT DEMAND IMMERSION

On Monday evening, after an early Supper, William and Dora hastened to the parsonage. Dora preferred to remain at home, but at her husband's earnest insistence she accompanied him.

They found Mr. C. ready to receive them. After mutual greetings, William, impatient for the discussion, said: "I have come, according to promise, to have that conversation on the subject of baptism. And I tell you candidly, I am so thoroughly convinced that immersion is the only true mode of baptism, that I do not believe it possible for you to convince me that your mode will at all meet the requirements of the Savior's command. But as I am so anxious to unite with your church, that I may be with my wife, and as you so positively refuse to immerse me, I thought I would beg an interview, to see if you have anything new to advance on this oft-disputed question. But first, let me ask you why you refuse to immerse me."

PASTOR.– "I am glad you have come. A free conversation on the subject can result in no harm, even if, as you think probable, I fail to convince you that we have any warrant from the Word of God for our mode of administering the rite of baptism. I am glad of the opportunity of answering the question you put so pointedly, especially as some are inclined to think we are not as consistent as we might be in some of our practices concerning baptism. I am glad you assumed that, as I refused to immerse you, I have a reason for such refusal. I have a reason, and I am very happy to give it. It is because I do not believe that immersion is the scriptural mode of baptism."

W.– "I certainly do not understand you. I thought you held to the view that immersion is not essential, but that it is a scriptural mode."

P.– "If this were my view, I would, most cheerfully, comply with your request. I refused because, as I said, I do not believe that immersion is a scriptural mode of administering baptism. It fails in essential points to meet the requirements of baptism, as instituted and appointed by Christ."

W.– "Well, this is certainly something new. On last Sabbath I heard Mr. R. give, as, to my mind, a strong argument in favor of immersion, that all denominations regard it as valid. But how will you reconcile such a theory with your practice? You offered to receive me on immersion, and suggested to me that I should get Mr. R. to immerse me, and then come to you with a certificate of membership, on which you would receive me."

P.– "Yes, sir, it is our custom to receive any one from an evangelical church applying for membership, on his immersion, if he is entirely satisfied with that as baptism."

W.– "Well I confess this seems to me irreconcilable. Valid, yet not scriptural; not scriptural, yet valid. If you can succeed in reconciling these contradictories to my satisfaction, I will think it possible you may force me to modify my views on the question of mode."

P.— "I hope the task will not be difficult. If they are, as you say, logical contradictions, of course they are irreconcilable, and it follows, as some think, that our theory and practice are inconsistent. But let me ask you what you understand by valid?"

W.— "I mean that which may be received as meeting the requirements of the gospel and the commands of Christ."

P.— "Very good. But perhaps we can understand each other better by considering validity as it relates to some other things. Allow me to inquire what you regard as the scriptural mode of administering and celebrating the Lord's Supper?"

W.— "I believe the mode practiced in your church is according to Christ's appointment."

P.— "Then it is scriptural?"

W.— "Yes, sir, I believe it is."

P.— "As instituted by Christ and celebrated by the apostles, is it probable that they kneeled in partaking of the elements?"

W.— "No, sir. It is certain they did not; and I confess I always regarded that mode of celebrating the ordinance as of questionable propriety, and as having no warrant from the Word of God."

P.— "As unscriptural?"

W.— "Yes, sir, as unscriptural."

P.— "And did it strike you that this destroyed its character as the Lord's Supper, and should not be regarded as such by those who agree with you?"

W.— "Well, no; not exactly that; but it is a departure from the simplicity of the ordinance as instituted by Christ, and has no warrant in the Scriptures."

P.— "I think I understand you. Though it be unscriptural, yet it may be valid."

W.— "I confess it is so in this case. But in giving and receiving the bread and wine, they retain the essentials of the Supper."

P.— "Very true; and so do immersionists, in using water in baptism, retain the essential element, but are without any scriptural warrant in their mode of using it. But this does not necessarily render their baptism invalid. But though I may regard it as valid, yet it would be wicked in me to do deliberately what I regard as unscriptural."

W.— "I admit your argument seems conclusive; but can you give another illustration as much to the point?"

P.— "Any number you desire, limited only by the number of externals in religious service. In externals God looks upon the heart, and considers the spirit in which the service is rendered. Let me ask what you regard as the scriptural Sabbath?"

W.— "Sunday, by universal consent."

P.— "Would it be proper or scriptural for you or the church to change it to any other day without a Divine warrant?"

W.— "On no account would it be admissible."

P.— "The case is a possible one, and let us suppose it, that a pious man or family should lose the day of the week. He is a farmer in a thinly-settled region. The Sabbath comes, and they all engage in their usual work. According to their count, Monday is the Sabbath, and as such it is religiously observed. It is conceivable that such a state of things might continue for many weeks. In his ignorance he has actually changed the divinely appointed day of rest. It is, as all will admit, unscriptural to substitute Monday for the day appointed by Christ; yet will not his observance of Monday, under the circumstances, meet all the requirements of the gospel?"

W.— "It is very plain. You have reconciled what I deemed irreconcilable. I can now better understand the language of the Savior when He said: 'God is spirit, and those who worship him must worship in spirit and truth.'[1] I can see that in things purely external God will have regard to the intention and the spirit in which the duty is attended to."

P.— "Another case, very analogous to our reception, from evangelical churches, of those who have been immersed, is where irregularities have occurred in the ordination of church officers. We believe that elders should be ordained by 'the laying-on of hands.'[2] To set them apart to their work without this formality would be unscriptural. But suppose that, through inadvertence (the thing has occurred), the imposition of hands should be neglected, and the elder, as thus ordained, should enter upon his official duties. If, some time afterwards, attention should be called to the omission— the irregularity— should the ordination be declared invalid, and all his official acts null and void?"

W.— "By no means. The case is analogous. I see how you are justified in receiving those who have been immersed, and yet refusing to administer the rite by immersion, just as you would, very properly, receive as valid an ordination unscriptural in form, as you have indicated, yet it would be wicked for you knowingly to assist in an ordination of the same kind."

P.— "Thus you see how I may receive one who has been immersed, yet it would be wicked in me to immerse him."

W.— "I see it. But I cannot express my astonishment to learn that you regard immersion as an unscriptural mode of baptism. You will find but few who will agree with you in that extreme view."

---

[1] John 4:24.
[2] 1 Timothy 5:22.

P.— "Immersionists are zealous in their labors to make such an impression, but it is very erroneous. The ministers of our Church, as a body, agree with me. A few, regarding it as a mere external, look upon it with such supreme indifference that they can scarcely be said to have an opinion on it; and such may sometimes make concessions which our opposers are very quick to catch up and use to their own advantage. I have known a few who would push this question of indifference to such an extreme that, while unhesitatingly declaring immersion unscriptural as a mode of baptism, would yet, on request, administer the rite in that way. The Presbytery of Lafayette, in answer to a memorial, declared by a unanimous vote that 'it is inexpedient and improper for a Presbyterian minister to administer the rite of baptism by immersion.'"

W.— "Such facts are new to me. But are you not mistaken as to the number of those who make such concessions? I have heard many sermons on the subject by immersionists, and by their quotations and statements they succeeded in making the impression on me that all Pædobaptists[3] agree in concessions that would seem to render the further discussion of the question unnecessary."

P.— "Such concessions form the burden of their books and sermons on the subject. Some years ago I put myself to some trouble to hear a Baptist minister, who proposed to discuss the subject purely from a Bible standpoint. I was anxious to know what a man could say in favor of immersion, in three sermons an hour each, who would confine himself to the Bible, and let Greek lexicons and Pædobaptist concessions alone.

"A worthy Baptist minister introduced the services by an earnest prayer, the burden of which was praise to God for His Word, for the clearness of its revelations, and its sufficiency in all things. I

---

[3] The prefix "pædo" means "child" or "infant;" for example, this is the origin of the title "Pediatrician."

was delighted with the prayer; I regarded it as a prelude to a Bible discussion, and thought that a desire, long entertained, to hear such a discussion, was about to be gratified.

"A gospel song was sung, and the minister, with only the open Bible before him, began his task. For about fifteen minutes I was charmed with an eloquent eulogy on the Bible. It was in the spirit of the prayer that preceded it. The massive Book, with its pages opened, was held up to our gaze; and 'here,' said the speaker, 'not in Creeds and Confessions of Faith, but here, in the Word of God, are we to look to find the mind of the Lord. To *the law* and the *Testimony*— if they speak not according to this word, *it is because there is no light in them.*

"What more could I desire? A Bible discussion of baptism! What I had so longed to hear.

"As the sound of the speaker's voice (in giving the quotation) was dying away, in a most reverent manner he gently closed the sacred volume, and with as much reverence as the case would admit of, he slowly pushed the source of light to his extreme left, taking one step to enable him to get it sufficiently far. The movement was inexplicable. But, in less time than it requires to tell you, the speaker was almost hidden behind books, large and small, which he piled before him and on his right and left.

"And now the Bible discussion!! For two hours we were treated to a learned dissertation— by one who knew nothing of the Greek language— on the meaning of '*baptidzo.*' Greek lexicons and Pædobaptist commentators and writers were the sole witnesses. The Bible was wholly ignored. It was not mentioned once. No text was quoted from it!!

"If it had been but a human production, I could but pity it on account of such treatment. Sacred volume, lifted so high to fall so low!

"My disappointment was great, but I went to hear the second and third discourses, 'et ab uno, disce omnes.'[4] The discussion of the subject, in all, occupied more than five hours, and only at the close, and then only for about fifteen minutes, did the Bible receive any notice, and then all that was done was to quote a few favorite passages, taking it for granted that they were conclusive in favor of immersion, but making no attempt at proof."

W.– "In all the books I have read on the subject, and in all the discussions to which I have listened, I have noticed that such was their method, and I think it proper. It served to establish me in my views. With such concessions, and the plain teachings of the Bible, I have come to regard the question as removed from debatable ground, and I cannot express to you my astonishment that you would intimate that a Pædobaptist would undertake to uphold his views from the Bible alone! Am I correct in drawing the inference that anyone would undertake such a task?"

P.– "Do you think any other method legitimate and satisfactory?"

W.– "I certainly think such a method best; but I see no objection to other aids, especially to the *ad hominem*[5] arguments to which you have referred."

P.– "I think you have very properly characterized those arguments as ad hominem. But let me ask you if such arguments, based on the concessions of some, prove anything, or establish any truth?"

W.– "Well, no. But they silence the opponents who make them."

P.– "Very true; but should not such discussions have, for their chief end, the establishment of the truth, and not the silencing of an opponent that may have been long dead?"

W.– "It is even so; but such arguments are equally valid against those who receive their writings."

---

[4] Latin, translated: "from one person, learn all people."
[5] An *ad hominem* argument is an argument "to the man," that is, a personal attack instead of an address of the reason and evidence presented.

P.– "But our reception of their writings in general does not imply that we accept of their concessions. Of what use, then, to thrust such concessions at us? They may please those already convinced, and make an impression on the unthinking, but are utterly valueless as a means of bringing to light the truth."

W.– "There is force in what you say; but I suppose they regard the teachings of the Bible on the subject so plain as not to claim, at any length, their attention, and all these arguments are so much extra."

P.– "Now I will answer a question you propounded some time ago, that is, whether you were to infer, from what I said, that any one, holding to my views on this subject, would undertake its discussion solely from the Bible standpoint?"

W.– "Yes, sir, if you please. I am curious to hear your answer to that question."

P.– "My answer is an emphatic *yes*. In the language already quoted, 'to the teaching and to the testimony! If they will not speak according to this word, it is because they have no dawn.'"[6]

W.– "My feelings are as you described your own, when you put yourself to the trouble of going to hear a Bible discussion on this subject. It will, I assure you, be a treat to me to hear one, confining himself to the Bible alone, attempt to meet and oppose the arguments in favor of immersion, and to give a 'thus says the LORD,' in favor of sprinkling."

P.– "And I can assure you it will give me much pleasure to gratify you. But I think it is better to postpone the further consideration of the subject until it is convenient for you to call again."

W.– "I hope you will permit me to call at an early period, for I can convey to you no idea of the extent to which my curiosity has

_____

[6] Isaiah 8:20.

been excited by what you have said, or rather by what you propose to say. Allow me the privilege of giving expression to my curiosity, and do not regard me as intending anything discourteous; but really, sir, it strikes me as so odd: the river Jordan to be dried up, the whole theory of immersion to be overturned, and sprinkling to be established, and by the Bible only!"

P.– "No offense, I assure you, by such expressions of your emotions. Allow me, however, to correct one false impression. I do not propose to dry up the Jordan, but instead of a work so miraculous, I will show you how God's people can be baptized on dry land, as the Israelites were in crossing the Red Sea. If it suits your convenience, you can return on Thursday evening. I shall await your return with interest, and hope to gratify your curiosity until it is satisfied."

W.— "*Excuse* me for making my appearance so early, but my curiosity has not abated. I saw Mr. R., and told him of my interview with you. He made a suggestion to me, which I had thought of before, and of which I had before spoken to my wife. I ask you for your opinion, and hope, in giving it, you will lay aside all prejudice, remembering that the religious interests of myself and wife are involved in it; remember that it is a matter that should rise above denominational preferences. I will say nothing more to my wife about it unless you agree with me that it is proper. It is this, that it would require less sacrifice on the part of my wife to go with me to the Baptist church, than for me to become a Presbyterian, especially as you refuse to immerse me."

P.— "I am glad you came so early, and equally glad that your interest is not abated. The suggestion of Mr. R. affords an opportunity of showing how inexcusably blind some people choose to be. I thank you for your confidence in my ability to express an opinion in the light of those interests which are immeasurably above denominational preferences. I will answer you as I believe my Master would have me answer. You believe your wife to be an honest, intelligent Christian woman?"

W.— "Without a superior in all these respects."

P.— "As an intelligent member of the Presbyterian Church, she believes that she has been baptized according to the command of Christ. Let me put a case in many respects analogous, that will serve as an illustration. Some twelve years ago Mr. L, a nominal Catholic, was united in marriage to Miss D., a member of the Presbyterian Church. The ceremony was performed by a Presbyterian minister. Matters went on smoothly for some three or four years, until Mr. L. became a very zealous Catholic. After he came entirely under the control of the priest, the latter told him that he was not lawfully married, and that he was committing a great sin to continue in that state. The poor man was in great trouble. The priest insisted that he should be married according to the laws of the church. The wife was informed of the trouble, and asked to assent to the arrangement. Her answer was prompt and emphatic. It was, 'no, never!' She saw that it would, in a most aggravating manner, cast contempt on the claims of her own church. It would be acknowledging that it was an apostate church, and its ministers impostors, without any authority to solemnize a marriage. It would be a confession that she had, for these years, been living in adultery. What think you of her conclusions and her answer?"

W.— "She was a noble, honest, Christian woman."

P.— "And what would be the confession of your wife, should she heed the suggestion of Mr. R., and apply to the Baptist Church for admission, and by him be immersed? It would be a confession of one or the other of these things: 1st, That her church is no church, and its ministers without any authority to administer the sacraments, and thus pour contempt on those she was leaving; or 2nd, If she held no such views as these, she would, by her act, pour contempt on the sacrament of baptism, regarding it as a thing so common, of so little worth, that it could be prostituted to the low work of ministering to the whims of a man she loved."

W.— "I see how I was blinded. I see how grievous would be my wife's offense to take that step I so desire her to take. I would not give my consent for her to make the change, unless her views on the subject of baptism should undergo a radical change."

P.— "I am rejoiced to hear you so express yourself. Before proceeding to the task before us, let us have a clear understanding of the work to be done. Allow me to ask what you understand by baptism, or immersion?"

W.— "It is very simple. It is putting the person down into the water, and taking him up out of the water, all in the name of the Father, the Son, and the Holy Spirit."

P.— "Very good. Another question. Would it meet the requirement if a quantity of water sufficient to cover the person should be poured upon him?"

W.— "Not at all. The action would be wanting. There would be no immersion; no putting down into, and taking up out of."

P.— "Of course your answer is correct. The whole difference between us and immersionists is not in the element to be employed; in this we agree; nor in the quantity to be employed, but in the action or in the use or application of the element. With immersionists it is, the individual must be put into the element; with us it is, the element must be applied to the individual. The difference is radical. Both cannot be right, because they are logical contraries. Now, I suppose, we can enter upon the consideration of the question?"

W.— "Yes, sir; with the distinct understanding that the Bible only is to be brought forward as a witness. No Greek, no commentaries, no doubtful historical tomes. But I suppose this is your understanding, as I see you are provided with a single volume, and that, I presume, is the Bible."

P.— "Pardon me, sir, but I fear you have misinterpreted my statement. I said nothing about the Greek. I proposed to confine myself exclusively to the Bible. A portion of the Scriptures was written in the Greek language, and the whole Bible was in that language when the Savior was on earth, and received His sanction. The meaning of the word employed to designate the rite is to be determined by its use in the Bible, and that cannot be done without some reference to the original text."

W.— "My meaning was that you would not bother me with learned citations from classic Greek authors, and long disquisitions on Greek prepositions."

P.— "And that was my meaning also. The only proper way to ascertain the meaning of a word of frequent occurrence in any volume is to note carefully how it is used in the several places where it occurs."

W.— "I do not believe I understand you. It seems to me that the best way to ascertain the meaning of a word in any language is to appeal to the dictionaries of acknowledged authority in that language. Or, if a derivative, to take advantage of this to get at its meaning."

P.— "By the latter method we might be led into error. Our word 'prevent' will serve as an illustration. It is derived from the Latin preposition 'prae,' meaning 'before,' and 'venire,' 'to come.' The word then should mean 'to come before.' But in this sense it has long been obsolete. Words undergo very material changes in their meaning. The word 'telegraph' may be cited as an example of such changes. Its meaning now is distinctly understood by all. To use it as it was understood forty years ago, very few would understand it. Then it meant to communicate at considerable distances by beacons. As to dictionaries, allow me to ask you how their compilers obtain their information? Take any standard dictionary of our own language; examine and see by what means the definitions are obtained. Here is Webster's Unabridged; examine any important word."

W.– "I see an illustration of your meaning in the definition given to the word 'presence.' Definitions are given, and following each are quotations from Milton, Shakespeare, Bacon, Dryden, and Collier. I see the same in many other definitions. I had often noticed such quotations, but their particular use had never struck me."

P.– "If you would take the trouble to examine a dictionary of any dead language, you would find a still greater use of this method. The lexicographer assigns a particular meaning to a word. In proof that such is its meaning, he quotes from some standard author a passage in which the word occurs. That the author so employed the word, is to be ascertained from the context and circumstantial evidence."

W.– "That certainly is a legitimate conclusion; confine yourself to that, and prove that the disputed word does not mean immerse, and I am satisfied."

P.– "In such an investigation, of course, we need examine only those passages where the context, or attending circumstances will throw some light on the meaning of the word as used by the writer. Thus, in the commission, 'Go therefore and make disciples of all nations, baptizing them in the name of the Father and of the Son and of the Holy Spirit,'[1] though the word occurs, yet the context affords no clue to its meaning. Again, there are many passages where the word occurs from which no conclusion can be drawn without involving a long and tedious discussion as to the signification of certain Greek prepositions. A few

---

[1] Matthew 28:19.

examples will suffice, 'John baptized with water.'[2] The meaning of the word, as here used, depends on the signification of the preposition translated 'with.' The inference from the English would be that the water was applied to them. Again, 'Jesus... was baptized by John in the Jordan.'[3] The simple fact here stated determines nothing as to the meaning of the word. They may have gone into the water, and then performed the rite either by dipping or sprinkling. Such passages must be examined under another head."

W.— "Do not the circumstances attending the baptism of Jesus— a part of which you quoted— and the passage giving an account of the baptism of the Eunuch,[4] all point to immersion?"

P.— "After we have considered the meaning of the word, we propose to examine the most important cases of its administration, reaching a conclusion as to the mode from the attending circumstances. Our present object is to look for passages where the use of the word clearly indicates its meaning. Will you turn to Daniel 4:25?"

W.— "It says that Nebuchadnezzar shall be wet with the dew of heaven."

P.— "The word translated wet is similar to the word used to designate the rite of baptism. Here, as the context will show you, Nebuchadnezzar was in the field, eating grass as a beast, making the open field his dwelling— his lodging place, as did the cattle. Yet here he was to be baptized; and the method is given; it should be by the dew of heaven.

"Another passage is Mark, 7:4: 'and when they come from the marketplace, they do not eat unless they wash. And there are many other traditions that they observe, such as the washing

---

[2] Acts 1:6; cf. Acts 11:16.
[3] Mark 1:9.
[4] See Acts 8:27-39.

[baptism] of cups and pots and copper vessels and dining couches.' Here the very word used to designate the rite of baptism is employed— 1st, in reference to the Jews themselves; 2nd, in reference to articles of household furniture, tables or couches. In the first case it is declared, every time they came from the market they baptized. It is conceivable that they might have immersed themselves, but it requires an effort of the imagination to regard it as probable. Obviously, what they desired to accomplish was to purify, cleanse themselves. This we know they were in the habit of doing."

W.— "You acknowledge that it is conceivable that they may have immersed themselves. Then I do not see how the word, as it occurs, can serve your purpose."

P.— "If you will turn to John 2:6, you will find an account of the provision they made for these purifications. We have here a detailed account of Christ's miracle, turning water into wine, at the marriage in Cana. In the 6th verse we read, 'Now there were six stone water jars there for the Jewish rites of purification, each holding twenty or thirty gallons.' According to some, these water-pots held about ten gallons each. The very highest is twenty-seven gallons each. According to the first, Christ made about one hogshead[5] of wine; according to the largest estimate, he made nearly three hogsheads. If we take the largest estimate, i.e., twenty-seven gallons each, such a vessel could not by any means have met the requirements for immersion."

W.— "I will take a note of this. I confess the comparison of these passages presents a point to which my attention has never before been called."

P.— "The case of the 'tables' or 'couches' is very conclusive; for it would require a power of imagination possessed by few to conceive that they were immersed. Two facts render it certain

---

[5] A hogshead is a common measure of wine amounting to 63 gallons, or 238.48 liters.

that they were not immersed: 1st, their size. It matters not whether we understand the word to refer to tables on which food was placed, or to couches on which they reclined when eating. In either case they were so cumbersome as to render it morally certain that housewives were not in the habit of immersing them. 2nd, no sensible reason can be assigned why they would want to immerse them. Simple immersion is not a method of cleansing anything. True, housewives do sometimes immerse 'cups' and 'pots' in the process of cleansing; but such immersion is a mere accidental circumstance; the method commonly employed is the free application of water and rubbing them, or by partial dipping; but in cleansing chairs, or benches, or tables, who ever heard of immersing them?"

W.— "I freely admit that in the case of Nebuchadnezzar, and in the example quoted from Mark's Gospel, there was no immersion proper. I do not suppose any one would for a moment contend there was. But I certainly lose nothing by such a concession, for I know your good sense and honesty will compel you to make a concession that will fully counterbalance mine."

P.— "I thank you for your expressions of confidence in me."

W.— "Admitting that these were not cases of literal, real immersion; yet was not Nebuchadnezzar, so to speak, enveloped in or with the moisture? And were not the tables or couches, being washed all over, in a like manner enveloped? And might not this, in a figurative sense, be considered a baptism or immersion? The end was attained, at least figuratively, that is, their envelopment."

P.— "I will readily make the concession you desire, on one condition, that is, that we regard this as one point fixed, agreed upon, and to which we may both refer as established."

W.— "The condition is a fair one, and I accept it."

P.— "Allow me to call your attention to one of your definitions. I urged you to define immersion, as without such definition all discussion would be useless."

W.— "I intended my definition to apply to the administration of the rite, or to real immersion."

P.— "And our object now is to find out the meaning of the word used to designate the rite. It would seem, then, that the word is used in the Bible to designate an action very different from putting down in and taking up out of."

W.— "You make a point that I will have to think about. I am not now prepared to express an opinion."

P.— "Well, think about it, and let me make another point, which you may perhaps associate with it for company. Allow me to apply to you the expressions of honesty and good sense by which you honored me. If the dew of heaven could baptize Nebuchadnezzar, and the application of water to tables could baptize them, as you say, figuratively, then you will acknowledge that should I take a hyssop branch, or my hand, and sprinkle a bountiful supply of water over an individual, so that he would, so to speak, be enveloped thereby, this would also be figurative immersion or baptism."

W.— "This does, indeed, look like a fit companion to the other point. Perhaps I was hasty in that agreement."

P.— "You are at liberty to regard it as null and void."

W.— "But I do not see that I would gain anything thereby."

P.— "Why not?"

W.— "Because I would then be driven to the necessity of acknowledging that real baptism, according to the Bible use of the word, could be performed when there is no immersion, but only the application of water to the person or thing to be baptized."

P.– "I am glad you see the point so clearly, and thank you for saving me the trouble of pressing it. I could not have made it better."

W.– "I confess, sir, that I am quite perplexed. From my early boyhood I have taken a deep interest in this question: I have discussed it, heard it discussed, read about it, and my mind was so fixed that I did not think it possible that anything that could be advanced could cause any hesitation or wavering on my part. I scarcely know why I sought these interviews with you. It was not certainly from any thought that you could convince me that my views are erroneous. I rather secretly indulged the hope that I could convince you of error, and at least induce you to immerse me. But why is it that I have never seen these points presented as they have been by you?"

P.– "I suppose it is because your reading has all been on one side of the question, or because you would not attend to anything on the opposite side."

W.– "Do not understand me as acknowledging for one moment that my views on this subject are erroneous. Whatever may be true of the occasional use of the word in a figurative sense, yet the cases of immersion recorded in the New Testament, and the fact that it is called a burial, are sufficient to settle the question with me."

P.– "Those cases of its administration are yet to be considered; also the passages which you claim as a warrant for believing it to symbolize a burial. But let us consider one thing at a time. We are now considering the use of the word in passages that clearly indicate its signification."

W.– "I am satisfied it is sometimes used in a figurative sense, as you have shown, and other examples will not make that more apparent; and besides, I am impatient to hear what you have to say of baptism as a burial."

P.— "We will examine that to your satisfaction in its proper place and time. As to the use of the word, it is true one clear example is as conclusive as a score. But I want you to see that we are not confined to a single obscure passage to ascertain the Bible use of the word. In Matthew 20:22, Jesus, in answer to the request of two of his disciples, to sit the one on his right hand and the other on his left in his kingdom, asked, 'Are ye able to drink of the cup that I drink of, and to be baptized with the baptism that 1 am baptized with? And when they said they were able, he said, 'You shall be baptized with the baptism that I am baptized with.'"[6]

W.— "Another figurative use of the word."

P.— "Very true. But it shows how the sacred writers were accustomed to use the word. To what, think you, did the Savior refer by this baptism?"

W.— "Obviously to his sufferings."

P.— "And is there an immersion here?"

W.— "I think you are unfortunate in the selection of this passage for your purpose, for I have often heard of the expression 'immersed in business, immersed in trouble.' I think it a very proper use of the term as referring to the troubles about to come upon him. Jesus was, so to speak, overwhelmed with trouble."

P.— "I think I understand you. You mean that trouble did not come on him in drops, but in a shower, or rather in a torrent."

W.— "That last word expresses the idea."

P.— "Then we are more nearly agreed in our views than we seemed to be at first. We do not differ as to the mode of baptism, but simply as to the quantity of the element that is to be employed."

---

[6] Matthew 20:23, as rendered in the King James version; note that more recent translations omit the language of baptism in the verses cited from Matthew. However, Mark's account of the same event includes the baptism language (Mark 10:38).

W.— "I see you will give me no rest about my definition of immersion."

P.— "At the outset we were agreed as to the element, and I wanted to know just wherein we differed; whether it was in reference to the quantity to be applied, or in the action. Will you now amend your answer?"

W.— "I would prefer to go to the consideration of the significance of the rite, and hear what you have to say about baptism as a burial."

P.— "As you seem so anxious for the consideration of that subject, I will now forewarn you that I will not leave a four-penny nail[7] to hold your scaffolding together when we come to consider the significance of the rite. I will not insist on an answer to my question, because I know you can give no definition of baptism by which you can stand.

"It has always been the practice of immersionists, in their interpretations of those passages where the word occurs, to swing backwards and forwards from action to quantity, and from quantity to action, just as it suited them. In the passages to which I have called your attention, they very clearly see immersion— that is, envelopment; that is, an extra quantity descending upon, but no action. If they would stick to this, we might make some compromise, and agree to the use of a greater quantity of the element, enough to represent an envelopment. But no sooner do we make a suggestion of such compromise than they tell us it is not quantity, but action; there must be a putting down into, and a taking up out of— a burial. Allow me to trouble you with another passage, found in Luke 11:38. Will you please read it?"

---

[7] Four-penny nails are the smallest size of true nails (brads and tacks are smaller still, but are not considered nails).

W.— "'The Pharisee was astonished to see that he did not first wash [baptize] before dinner.'"

P.— "The word here used is the very same applied to the rite of baptism. I will not trouble you to compare it with Mark 7:2-3, although a strong argument might easily be drawn from such comparison. In all candor ask yourself what could have been meant by the statement you have just read."

W.— "Candor compels me to admit that it could not have been used to indicate immersion. There could have been no use in it, and I imagine that it would have been practically impossible."

P.— "You take a common sense view of it. We keep up the same practice in reference to the first meal of the day. Except we baptize, we eat not our morning meal. I would like also to call your attention to a use of the word as found in Hebrews 9:10, from which a similar conclusion could be drawn. Also 1 Corinthians 10:1-2, where baptism is used to designate simply consecration, and no immersion can be found. But as you seem satisfied on this point, we will dismiss it, and pass to the consideration of that in which you seem to display so much interest; that is, the significance of the rite. But we must adjourn to another evening for the consideration of this."

49

Third Evening: Baptism and Burial

W.— "I have carefully examined the passages which occupied our attention during the last evening, and also had an interview with Mr. R. He told me the word found in Daniel is not the word used to designate the rite. He says there is a marked difference. I noticed the difference, one being *bapto*, and the other *baptidzo*. But I remember that some of my Baptist friends used to urge that there was no difference, and even that the former is the stronger of the two, as it is the root of the other."

P.— "This shows to what men will resort to accomplish a purpose. The same word occurs in Revelation, and is frequently translated 'to dip.' When used in such a sense it serves their purpose. If the word *baptidzo* means immerse, much more its root would signify a similar action. If it could be shown that *bapto* meant to dip or immerse, and nothing else, an opposer of immersion might, with some show of reason, protest against the conclusion that *baptidzo*, a derivative, should have the same intensive meaning. Derivatives are supposed to be used in a less intensive and restricted sense; but in these words they would reverse the order."

W.— "That is the view I took of it. But I did not give much attention to it, as it would avail nothing for the other passages you quoted. So if you are willing, we will pass to the symbolical nature of the rite, as you said this would occupy our attention this evening. In this I will feel more at home, and am certain I will be proof against any arguments you can offer.

P.— "I am glad you will feel at home in the consideration of this subject, but hardly know whether to commend your last statement, as it seems to imply —"

W.— "What I meant is that I have such authority from the word of God on the question of the significance of baptism, that nothing that any one can advance can effect any change in my views."

P.— " Perhaps it will be best to have a statement at your views on the subject— what you regard as symbolized by the rite."

W.— "I can give them, and the reasons for them in very few words. I look upon baptism as commemorative of the burial and resurrection of Jesus. Nearly all the ordinances of God are of this character. Circumcision is, I believe, an exception. They are designed to commemorate some mighty event which has transpired in his divine interposition in behalf of his people..... And so the Lord's Supper is commemorative of the death of our Lord Jesus Christ. But now, have we no commemorative rite for his burial and resurrection? We have not, unless baptism is that rite. Now, I cannot believe that God would be careful to provide for the commemoration of those other events, and then fail to make any provision for this. It may be said that, in comparison with this, the rest are quite insignificant. The resurrection of Christ is the mightiest event that has ever occurred. It is the basis of the Christian religion. It is the foundation of all our hopes. Remove it, and the whole structure of Christianity tumbles into ruins. A fact, then, so grand, and of such magnitude, and of such importance, could not be allowed to go without commemoration. And cannot that eye of faith which sees the broken body of Jesus in the broken loaf; which sees the warm blood flowing from his cleft side in the flowing wine, see the buried Savior in the immersion of one dead to sin; can it not see him risen in the emersion that follows?"

P.— "It is very clear that you are at home on this subject, and that you have given it careful attention; and from your emphasis it is no less evident that you feel the truth of what you affirm. This extended and clear statement of your views has somewhat changed my mind as to the order to be observed in the consideration of the subject. I agree with you in many of your statements; but may I ask what the burial of Jesus had to do with his great work for us?"

W.— "I am at a loss to know what you mean by such a question. It would seem to imply that it had nothing to do with his work as a Savior. Is this your meaning?"

P.— "It is. I am at a loss to see any purpose it serves in his mediatorial work. Allow me to ask what would have been the character of his work. if, having died as he did, about the ninth hour on Friday, his body had been left on the cross until Sunday morning, and then he had come back to life, and had come down from the cross?"

W.— "Burial is a proof of death. It shows that the Savior was certainly dead."

P.— "Do you think his burial was essential to prove that fact?"

W.— "Well, no; I cannot say that it was."

P.— "Will you, then, answer the question I propounded?"

W.– "I cannot see that it would have detracted from the value of his work. But his burial was intimately connected with his resurrection, and that, surely, had much to do with his work."

P.– "Do you mean that the essential part of his resurrection was his coming out of the tomb?"

W.– "It was his coming back to life."

P.– "And this he could have done if he had not been buried at all."

W.– "I never saw the subject presented in that light. But in any case his resurrection was a most important event– fully equaling in importance his death. And as all such great events should have something to commemorate them, this is left without commemoration, if this office is not performed by baptism."

P.– "I fully agree with you as to the importance of the resurrection – his coming to life again– not simply his coming out of the tomb; this was a matter of no consequence. I agree with you also as to the desirableness of having so great an event as his resurrection commemorated. But let us, for a moment, change the subject, and permit me to ask you what day of the week was observed as the Sabbath when Christ was on earth?"

W.– "I do not see the object of such digression, but I will answer you. It was Saturday."

P.– "And now what day is so kept?"

W.– "We observe Sunday."

P.– "And why the change?"

W.– "I see your point, but cannot evade an answer. The change was made because on this day Christ arose from the dead."

P.– "Then, that important event is not left un-commemorated."

W.– "No, sir; I never thought of it before, but it is really commemorated better than any other event connected with his work."

P.— "I would have you note the two facts thus brought to light: 1st, that the burial of Jesus had nothing whatever to do with his work in saving sinners. 2nd, that his resurrection is abundantly commemorated in the day we observe as the Sabbath."

W.— "But I am not satisfied with the conclusion to which you have come in reference to the burial of Christ. You have, apparently, demonstrated that it had nothing to do with our salvation, and therefore, needed no commemoration. Though I am unable to see it, and point it out, yet I know your conclusion involves some fallacy, because Paul says emphatically, that 'baptism symbolizes the burial of Jesus.'"

P.— "I suppose you refer to Romans 6:2-4?"

W.— "I do; and no language could be plainer."

P.— "Do not the facts already brought to light tend to create a suspicion in your mind as to the correctness of your interpretation of that passage?"

W.— "If his statement were not so plain, it might. But the reference is too natural and the language too plain to allow such a suspicion to suggest itself."

P.— "Perhaps, then, before examining the passage, it may be well to make a few inquiries in reference to its utterance. May I ask you where we meet with the first passage that, to your mind, seems to intimate that baptism has any reference to a burial, or to Christ's burial?"

W.— "This one in Romans and a similar one in Colossians[1] are the only ones that teach it clearly."

P.— "Is there nothing in the four Gospel histories, or in the Acts of the Apostles, from which you could draw such a conclusion?"

W.— "Nothing that I am aware of."

---

[1] Colossians 2:12.

P.– "And is Paul, in the sixth of Romans, discussing the subject of baptism in a didactic manner. Does the context intimate that his object is to supplement what Christ and his apostles had omitted, in the five books named, on this matter of baptism as a rite in the church?"

W.– "I cannot say that he does. He refers to it because it serves to illustrate a very important truth, which it does most perfectly, i.e., our death to sin."

P.– "Now, my friend, allow me to ask you what would you think or say if a fundamental peculiarity of our denomination was based on a passage of Scripture, written thirty or forty years after Christ's ascension, when the writer was not ostensibly intending to teach anything on the subject, but only referred to it incidentally, by way of illustrating a point having no direct bearing on the subject; when, too, we would search in vain the four Gospels and Acts for any warrant for our particular views; and when, in the whole Bible, except one similar reference, we could find no passage that suggested anything of the kind. What, under such circumstances, would you think or say?"

W.– "In general, I would say it was very presumptuous. But if the incidental reference was as plain as this one, I would be compelled to acknowledge your right to do so."

P.– "And suppose the passage admitted an interpretation entirely different from the one we gave it?"

W.– "Then your presumption would be without limits. But this one does not."

P.– "But a respectable portion of the Christian world says it does."

W.–"But they are mistaken."

P.– "Then I see we are not yet prepared to examine the passage. We must step aside, and examine it from a favorable standpoint.

W.–"By any method to reach the truth."

P.— "A few questions then. Was Christ buried?"

W.— "The Bible says so."

P.— "Will you give me the facts relating to his burial?"

W.— "He was taken down from the cross and laid in the new tomb of Joseph of Arimathea."

P.— "Please describe the tomb as well as you can."

W.— "It was hewn out of the rock."

P.— "And the burial, so far as the history enlightens us."

W.— "His body was carefully laid in this tomb and a stone was rolled against the door of it."

P.— "Would it have been materially different if they had taken the body to Joseph's house, and there placed it in a small room or apartment, and then closed the door?"

W.— "It was a sepulcher, and so spoken of."

P.— "Very good. But was it different, materially, from the case we have suggested as possible? Or if you do not like to answer that question, was the body at burial put down into the earth, and at the resurrection did it come up out of the earth?"

W.— "Let me hear your interpretation of the passage."

P.—"In a moment. Another question, if you please. Did the burial of Jesus have any resemblance to burial as we now perform that sad duty?"

W.— "Not much."

P.— "And suppose it had been precisely in accordance with our mode of burial, would it be aptly symbolized by immersion?"

W.— "It certainly would."

P.— "Immersion, then, is applying such a quantity of water to a person that by it he shall be hidden from view?"

W.— "They are covered; out of sight; buried."

P.— "The action, then, is nothing. The putting down in is not essential to immersion. It is enough if the element is put or poured on until the individual or object is covered."

W.— "Such a burial will answer as a figurative immersion."

P.— "And yet lack the essential part?"

W.— "But it is enough that Paul says, that baptism symbolizes the burial of Jesus."

P.— "There is one question to which I would like very much to get a candid answer. It is this: dismissing from your mind all notions of our modern mode of burial, and taking into consideration the simple facts related in the gospel history concerning the disposition that was made of the body of Jesus after the crucifixion; that he was laid in that little apartment hewn out of the solid rock; and supposing that this that was done with his body was to be symbolized with water, would the immersion of a person in water symbolize it any better than would sprinkling water upon him?"

W.— "I do not see that sprinkling would symbolize it at all."

P.— "Not even figuratively?"

W.—"It would strain one's imagination to see it."

P.— "Remember the baptism of Nebuchadnezzar with the dew of heaven; remember how often you have said that envelopment would answer all the requirements."

W.— "Do you imagine that sprinkling would serve to symbolize Christ's burial?"

P.— "Only by a stretch of the imagination that would he painful."

W.— "Then why do you put the question to me?"

P.— "My question is, would not sprinkling symbolize it as well as immersion?"

W.— "To be candid, I do not see that either will do it without some effort of imagination; but Paul says baptism does symbolize it?"

P.— "That is the question we will now consider. Let us first inquire what fact the apostle wishes to establish, or what point he wishes to make. Baptism is introduced as an illustration. Will you tell me what is the fact to be illustrated?"

W.— "He had stated that where sin abounded, there grace did much more abound. From this it might seem to follow, that as grace abounds most where sin abounds most, we may make, or let sin abound in order that grace may abound. To meet this monstrous conclusion, he says, 'How can we who *died* to sin still *live* in it?'[2] He then brings in the illustration, 'Do you not know that all of us who have been baptized into Christ Jesus were baptized into his death?'"[3]

P.— "I see you have a clear view of the connection, and of the point to be illustrated. In the passage last quoted, baptism is introduced twice; will you repeat the two things affirmed of it?"

W.— "First, we are baptized into Christ: second, we are baptized into his death."

P.— "Very good. What do you understand by the first?"

W.— "To get into Christ must mean to get into union with him, as we are so often said to be 'in Christ.' And to say that we are baptized into him is to affirm that, in some way, baptism secures this union."

P.— "You are an excellent theologian; and now for the second fact affirmed?"

---

[2] Romans 6:2.
[3] Romans 6:3.

W.— "I suppose that has a similar meaning. To be baptized into His death, must mean to come into union with it, so that, as by the first Christ becomes ours, so by the second his death becomes ours."

P.— "Very good, and a most important doctrine. Christ, as our Savior, must be seen in all things as our Substitute. His death was not, so to speak, a personal death; that is, it was not simply the death of the individual Christ Jesus. It was a representative death, or he died as representing us. Look on the cross, and tell me whom do you see there, forsaken of God, suffering and dying?"

W.— "I understand your meaning. We see God's people in the person of Jesus, their representative."

P.— "Then whose death was it?"

W.— "It was our death."

P.— "And by what means, according to the statement of the apostle, does his death become our death?"

W.— "By our union with him."

P.— "And how, according to his statement, is that union secured?"

W.— "By baptism: 'baptized into Christ.'"

P.— "And now the next statement."

W.— "'We were buried therefore with him by baptism into death, in order that, just as Christ was raised from the dead by the glory of the Father, we too might walk in newness of life.'"[4]

P.— "How is this verse introduced?"

W.— "By the participle 'therefore.'"

P.— "What does this mean?"

---

[4] Romans 6:4.

W.— "It shows us that it is an inference from the previous statement."

P.— "What do you understand by 'buried with?'"

W.— "I examined the passage in my Greek Testament, and found no word corresponding to the preposition 'with;' the verb is a compound, made up of the verb signifying 'to bury,' and the word signifying 'with,' or 'together with,' as a prefix. It means 'buried together with'; that is, both burials were one— the burial of Jesus and his people; they were buried together."

P.— "To be 'buried together with,' implies more than one person, and you say the reference is to 'Christ and his people.'"

W.— "That is clearly the meaning."

P.— "Then the apostle's statement is that, as Christ's death is our death, so his burial is our burial."

W.— "Such is his statement."

P.— "And how are we buried with him?"

W.— "The apostle says, 'by baptism.'"

P.— "Look again."

W.— "By baptism into death."

P.— "And do you think this statement is equivalent to 'by baptism into water?'"

W.— "I have always understood it as such."

P.— "But in the previous verse you had the expression, 'baptized into his death,' and you gave the only possible interpretation of it as it there stands. This second statement is an inference from that, which forewarns us that the apostle is about to apply the fact there stated. In the former statement, 'baptized into his death' means to be so united to him that his death becomes

61

ours. Here it must mean the same thing, and it must mean we are buried with him by being united to him."

W.— "That seems to be a legitimate inference, and the only possible interpretation."

P.— "But where is the reference to the mode of baptism?"

W.— "I always thought it was there, but this piecemeal method of interpretation obscures it. I confess I do not see it. But does not the apostle assign a peculiar office to baptism? He seems to speak of it as accomplishing or doing more than either of us would admit?"

P.— "Not at all. 'For there are three that testify: the Spirit and the water and the blood; and these three agree.'[5] What is true of the thing signified, may be, and often is, affirmed of the sign.

"No one would draw the monstrous conclusion from the statement of the apostle that water baptism unites us to Christ."

W.— "Then you do not think that the apostle here refers to water-baptism?"

P.— "Obviously the mode was not in his mind. What he said would have been just as appropriate of any rite intended to set forth what baptism does, that is, our union with Christ."

W.— "Explain your meaning."

P.— "Suppose, then, that circumcision had continued to be the rite of initiation into the church, and had signified our union with Christ. In such a case the same language could have been employed, substituting circumcision for baptism. It then would have been, 'Do you not know that all of us who have been circumcised into Christ [i.e., united to Christ by circumcision]

---

[5] 1 John 5:7-8.

Jesus were circumcised into his death? We were buried therefore with him by circumcision into death.'"[6]

W.— "I am not prepared to dispute the correctness of your interpretation; but I would like for you to explain how such a rite as circumcision could signify or symbolize the Spirit's work as baptism does?"

P.— "There is no doubt but that circumcision was intended to do that very thing. Frequently we read of 'circumcision of the heart.' Paul so understood it, as appears from this same Epistle to the Romans, at the close of the second chapter, where he so speaks of circumcision. 'For no one is a Jew who is merely one outwardly, nor is circumcision outward and physical. But a Jew is one inwardly, and circumcision is a matter of the heart, by the Spirit, not by the letter.'[7] This shows that circumcision had the same significance as baptism, i.e., the cleansing of the heart. And in the passage just quoted, the same kind of substitution can be made; that is, baptism for circumcision, and the same remains unchanged; 'that is not baptism which is merely one outwardly, but baptism is a matter of the heart, by the spirit, and not by the letter.'"

W.— "Though I am unable to show that your interpretation is not correct, yet it weakens my cause without strengthening yours."

P.— "How is that?"

W.—"Because it would then follow that the significance of the rite throws no light on the mode of its administration. But the undoubted examples of immersion recorded in the New Testament remain untouched and unanswerable."

P.— "As to your last statement, that remains to be considered. As to the first, I think you are laboring under a mistaken view of the subject. I think it capable of demonstration: 1st, that baptism

---

[6] Romans 6:3-4.
[7] Romans 2:28-29.

was not intended to symbolize nor commemorate a burial; 2nd, that it was intended to symbolize the work of the Spirit; 3rd, that this does throw light on the question of mode. The first we have already considered, and I hope to your satisfaction. The consideration of the other two statements we had better postpone until another evening."

FOURTH EVENING: SIGNIFICANCE OF BAPTISM

W.— "*You* treated our view of the significance of the rite of baptism in such a summary manner that I am anxious to hear what you have to say in favor of your own. It is easier to pull down than to build up."

P.— "I promise you that I will not rest our view on a passage written thirty or forty years after Christ's ascension, and in which baptism is only incidentally referred to, and that by way of illustrating a point having little connection, directly, with it."

W.— "The promise is fair if the fulfillment is as good."

P.— "A few words first, by way of introduction. Will you tell me how many persons of the Godhead have a part in the work of man's redemption?"

W.— "All of them. The Father sent the Son. The Son came and made atonement for sin. The Holy Spirit applies the benefit of Christ's work."

P.– "Very good. Will you mention a few things included in the Spirit's work."

W.– "The Spirit convinces of sin; inclines us to go to Jesus; regenerates and sanctifies us."

P.– "He has, then, a very important part to do in our salvation."

W.– "Equal to either of the others. The sacred writers frequently refer to his work."

P.– "Do you think his work is sufficiently important to merit a rite to commemorate or symbolize it?"

W.– "I certainly think it does, and I have always supposed that baptism does that in part."

P.– "And in a very small part according to your view; only in a very secondary manner."

W.– "Yes, our view is that baptism chiefly refers to the burial of Christ. But I have often wondered, as the Lord's Supper has exclusive reference to the work of Christ, why baptism did not have special reference to the work of the Spirit."

P.– "And a pity it is that you had not been led to pursue such inquiries to the extent of enabling you to see the whole truth. Allow me to put this case to you. Suppose you could find language like this, uttered, say, by John the Baptist: 'Christ shall be buried in the earth, but ye shall be buried by baptism in the water.' How could I, as an opposer of immersion, meet such a statement?"

W.– "You could not meet it at all. I wish such a statement had been left on record; it would have settled this question, and put an end to all discussion. But why do you put such a question? No such statement can be found."

P.– "I agree with you that it would have been conclusive. I ask the question that I may ask another. What would you say if you should find language like this: 'I have baptized you with water, but he will baptize you with the Holy Spirit.'"[1]

W.— "I remember that John did use this language, and I acknowledge that it points to an intimate connection between the work of the Spirit and water baptism."

P.— "And so it does. The great work of the Spirit is to cleanse, purify, and sanctify. Shall I quote passages in proof of this statement?"

W.— "No, it is not necessary. I remember several such."

P.— "On the other hand, water is the natural emblem of purifying, cleansing. Baptismal water is often so spoken of."

W.— "Yes, sir, I recollect passages that show this. It was said to Paul, 'rise and be baptized and wash away your sins.'"[2]

P.— "All such statements point us clearly to this fact, that the use of water in baptism is to commemorate or symbolize the work of the Spirit."

W.— "They do seem to indicate this. But it is frequently said that we are cleansed by Christ's blood. In the first Epistle of John it is said, 'the blood of Jesus his Son cleanses us from all sin.'"[3]

P.— "I am very much obliged to you for that suggestion and quotation. It might have been overlooked by me. Please turn to that same Epistle, chapter 5, verses 7 and 8, and read."

---

[1] Mark 1:8.
[2] Acts 22:6
[3] 1 John 1:7.

W.— "For there are three that testify: the Spirit and the water and the blood; and these three agree."[4]

P.— "Please emphasize that last clause."

W.— "'*And these three agree.*'"

P.— "What shall I now say in reference to your quotation from the first chapter, where it is said, the blood of Jesus cleanses from all sin?"

W.— "I see it. Both blood and water represent or symbolize the work of the Spirit. To all this I agree. But where does it lead us?"

P.— "Wait and see. We must pause here to examine a few passages in which the work of the Spirit is spoken of. I will select a few passages from the concordance, and ask you to read them. Here is one in Proverbs 1:23."

W.— "'If you turn at my reproof, behold, I will *pour out my Spirit* to you; I will make my words known to you.'"

P.— "Isaiah 32:15."

W.— "'Until the Spirit *is poured* upon us from on high, and the wilderness becomes a fruitful field, and the fruitful field is deemed a forest.'"

P.— "Isaiah 44:3."

W.— "'For I will *pour* water on the thirsty land, and streams on the dry ground; I will *pour my Spirit* upon your offspring, and my blessing on your descendants.'"

P.— "Ezekiel 39:29."

---

[4] As with the "Second Evening," the King James version includes language that modern translations do not include. In the original manuscript of *William the Baptist*, the verse quoted read as thus: " For there are three that bear record in heaven, the Father, the Word, and the Holy Ghost; and these three are one. And there are three that bear witness in earth, the Spirit, and the water, and the blood; and these three agree in one." However, in this case the difference between the King James and the modern translations does not affect the argument.

W.– "'And I will not hide my face anymore from them, when I *pour out my Spirit* upon the house of Israel, declares the Lord GOD.'"

P.– "Joel 2:28-29."

W.– "'And it shall come to pass afterward, that I will *pour out my Spirit* on all flesh; your sons and your daughters shall prophesy, your old men shall dream dreams, and your young men shall see visions. Even on the male and female servants in those days I will *pour out my Spirit*.'"

P.–"John 1:33."

W.– "'I myself did not know him, but he who sent me to baptize with water said to me, "He on whom you see *the Spirit descend* and remain, this is he who baptizes with the Holy Spirit."'"

P.– "Mark 1:10."

W.– "'And when he came up out of the water, immediately he saw the heavens being torn open and *the Spirit descending* on him like a dove.'"

P.– "Titus 3:6, and latter clause of 5th verse."

W.– "'...and renewal of the Holy Spirit, whom he *poured out on us* richly through Jesus Christ our Savior.'"

P.– "In Acts 2:16, you will find the passage from Joel quoted as fulfilled on the day of Pentecost, and remembering this will you please read the 33rd verse."

W.– "'Being therefore exalted at the right hand of God, and having received from the Father the promise of the Holy Spirit, he has *poured out* this that you yourselves are seeing and hearing.'"

P.– "Will you now tell me the various words used to express the gift or work of the Spirit in the passages read?"

W.— "So far as I recollect them, they are 'happen with,' 'poured upon,' 'poured out,'[5] 'descending on.'"

P.— "Do you recollect any passage in which the work of the Spirit is represented by anything like immersion?"

W.— "I was hoping you would ask me such a question; because there is a passage of that kind in a chapter from which you have quoted. It is the second of Acts, where the writer is speaking of the baptism of the Holy Spirit on the day of Pentecost, he says: 'And suddenly there came from heaven a sound like a mighty rushing wind, and it filled the entire house where they were sitting.'[6] Here it is stated, clearly, that they were entirely enveloped, or so to speak, buried."

P.— "So, then, though the Spirit was poured upon them, or descended upon them, yet if it was sufficiently extensive to envelop them, it was a baptism?"

W.— "In a figurative sense."

P.— "I am both sorry and glad that you have presented this case, and quoted this passage. Sorry, that one so intelligent should commit such a blunder. Glad, because others have done the same thing, and some notice should be taken of it. If you will examine the passage you will see that it says nothing about the Spirit filling the house. It was the sound that filled the house. In the third verse there is a description of the visible manifestation of the baptism by the Spirit. 'And divided tongues as of fire appeared to them and rested on each one of them.'"

W.— (After looking at the passage.) "Well, well, I am ashamed of myself, and thank you for the gentleness of the rebuke so kindly administered and so richly deserved. But I confess I never saw the passage in that light before. Many a time did I quote it as I

---

[5] In the original manuscript of *William the Baptist*, this word was "shed" which was more closely in accordance with the King James language.
[6] Acts 2:2.

did tonight, and regarded it as an excellent example of figurative immersion."

P.— "You must keep before your mind the points of difference between us. This you seem inclined to ignore when it suits your convenience. The whole question, as to the mode of baptism, is: Is the individual *put into the element?* Or is the element *applied to him?* To call that baptism where the element is applied to the individual in a quantity sufficient to envelop, is to decide that the difference in our views is not in the action or mode, but simply a difference in quantity. In that case, sprinkling must meet the requirement, if, like dew, it can be so applied as to represent an envelopment. Now what do you think baptism was intended to commemorate or symbolize?"

W.— "Clearly, the work of the Spirit."

P.— "And what light does it throw on the question of mode?"

W.— "I confess it does not seem to be very favorable to immersion. It does seem to point to baptism as consisting in the application of water to the individual. But all this offers no benefit for your side of the question, since the cases of its administration on record clearly point to the fact that immersion was the apostolic mode."

P.— "Those cases are yet to be examined. Perhaps they are not as decisive in favor of immersion as they seem to be from your standpoint."

W.— "The facts, the circumstances, are too plain to be mistaken. Could you succeed in convincing me to the contrary, it could only result in evil to me; for it would destroy my confidence in language. I would be compelled to believe that nothing can be stated in human language, but that it can be proved the writer meant no such thing."

P.— "The very fact that you can so speak shows how completely prejudice has blinded your eyes. In so speaking, you declare that all Pædobaptists are either liars or fools; either that they lack enough common sense to see these cases of immersion; or seeing them, they lack honesty to concede that they are such."

W.– "I beg your pardon, sir; but I did not mean to bring either of these charges against them. But will you not acknowledge that some cases of immersion are recorded in the New Testament?"

P.– "I will not acknowledge that the rite of baptism was so administered in any case recorded."

W.– "For you to attempt to prove such a statement to my satisfaction, is to undertake a task for which a dozen evenings would not suffice. But I am interested in the subject, and will come as often as need be to hear all you have to say."

P.– "I think one evening will be sufficient to say all that is necessary on the cases of its administration that are recorded in the New Testament. Whenever it suits your convenience, I shall be happy to consider them."

W.— "I have taken the trouble to read the account of the administration in several cases, and I think they are as clear and definite as I could give an account of immersion as now administered at any of our baptisms, and your time will be lost in attempting to convince me to the contrary. I cannot help but think, if language is to be trusted, we must believe that Jesus was immersed by John the Baptist in the Jordan; and the eunuch was immersed by Philip."

P.— "And are these all the examples or cases of its administration recorded in the New Testament?"

W.— "They are all that I examined, and they are enough."

P.— "Before considering any of these cases of its administration, let us distinctly understand each other as to the method of proceeding."

W.— "Will you please explain your meaning?"

P.– "I mean that we are now about to examine these cases to see what light, if any, they throw on the question of mode."

W.– "This is my understanding."

P.– "The evidence thus cited is what is called probable or circumstantial evidence. And in thus examining the recorded cases, it will be necessary to exclude every other kind of evidence. I mean it will be necessary for both of us, for the sake of argument, to admit that the evidence from the meaning of the word and the significance of the rite is equal on both sides. In other words, we are to suppose we have no kind of evidence as to the mode, except what is derived from the circumstances and facts recorded in connection with each case."

W.– "That would be the only fair way to proceed in such an investigation."

P.– "Then we are ready to proceed. It was my intention to introduce the subject in a manner somewhat different; but as your mind seems filled with thoughts of the cases you mentioned, perhaps it will be well to consider them at once."

W.– "If you please; if it makes no special difference to you, I would like for you to take up the case of the immersion of Jesus in the Jordan by John."

P.– "Perhaps it would be well to say the baptism of Jesus in the Jordan."

W.–"Just as you please; they are both the same to me."

P.– "May I ask you why John baptized, and what was the nature or object of his baptism?"

W.–" John baptized because God sent him to baptize, as John himself tells us. As to the object of his baptism, he said, 'I baptize you with water for repentance.'"[1]

---

[1] Matthew 3:11; cf. Luke 3:16.

P.– "And what does 'for repentance' mean?"

W.– "I suppose the meaning is, that baptism was to show them that they were sinful, needed cleansing, and should repent of their sins."

P.– "And how was it with Jesus?"

W.– "Of course, in his case, it was different. He, himself, tells us why he was baptized, and the object of it. 'Thus,' said he 'it is fitting for us to fulfill all righteousness.'"[2]

P.– "And what does he mean by 'righteousness.'"

W.– "I think I am prepared to answer that question, as I have just been studying the first five chapters of Romans, where this word frequently occurs. Dora and I were very much interested it. I had occasion to study this word particularly. It is a legal term, and different from holiness, as the latter relates to inward purity, and the former has reference to our relation to the law; doing what the law directs."

P.– "I admire your skill in interpretation. I do not see how your answer could be improved. It would seem, then, that there was some law making it necessary for Christ to he baptized."

W.– "It would seem so from this language; but I never examined into the matter, and I am not very familiar with the Old Testament Scriptures."

P.– "The baptism of Jesus is interesting and important for other reasons, different from those for which we are now examining it. As some of these facts are necessary for a clear understanding of this, I will mention them: Jesus is, emphatically, our Great High Priest. He is the only real priest that ever was in the world. Aaron's priesthood was typical of his, so that Aaron and his descendants may be called typical priests, and Christ the real priest. The Aaronic priesthood all pertained to the tribe of Levi,

[2] Matthew 3:15.

and were the descendants of Aaron. But Jesus belonged to another tribe, 'from which,' as Paul says, 'no one has ever served at the altar. For it is evident that our Lord was descended from Judah, and in connection with that tribe Moses said nothing about priests.' Hebrews 7:13-14, and in verse twelve, he says, 'For when there is a change in the priesthood, there is necessarily a change in the law as well.' Now, when the Aaronic priesthood was first instituted, the tribe to which it pertained was, in a formal manner, consecrated, set apart to this high calling. Whether, in subsequent ages, every priest was thus set apart, as he entered on his priestly office, it does not appear. But when so great a change occurred as Paul speaks of, a change to another tribe of which Moses said nothing about priests, then the law of consecration should be complied with; and it was to this law that Jesus referred in the language used by him."

W.— "Your statements are interesting and instructive, and I see very clearly that it was to such a law that he referred when he said, 'Thus it is fitting for us to fulfill all righteousness.'"[3]

P.— "If the means or mode of consecration in that first instance could be ascertained, it would afford light on the second; i.e., the consecration of Jesus, his conforming to the law, and thus fulfilling 'all righteousness.'"

W.— "I wish it had been given in detail. It would have thrown light upon, and perhaps settled this question, that has caused so much wrangling among the people of God."

P.— "That is a good wish; and I am happy to inform you that the method of consecration has been carefully preserved in the sacred records. Will you please turn to Numbers 8:5-7, and read?"

W.— "'And the LORD spoke to Moses, saying, "Take the Levites from among the people of Israel and cleanse them. Thus you

---

[3] Ibid.

shall do to them to cleanse them: *sprinkle the water of purification upon them.'*"

P.— "That is the law which Christ said he must obey to fulfill all righteousness."

W.— "Is it certain that he had reference to this law?"

P.— "It is *certain*, according to his own words, that there was some law with which he must comply.

"Again, it is *certain* that in complying with the law, it involved the use of water.

"Again, it is *certain* that he felt that he must comply with that law, because he was about entering upon his priestly work, not as a descendant of Aaron, or of the tribe of Levi, but as a member of another tribe— Judah.

"Again, it is *certain* that the law quoted was for the very purpose for which Jesus wished to be baptized.

"Again, it is *certain* that if this is not the law to which referred, then no such law was in existence.

"Again, it is *certain* that if there was no such law on record, there would have been no propriety in Jesus saying it was necessary for him to be baptized to comply with the law.

"And the seventh thing *certain* is, that he referred to this law."

William listened very attentively to the pastor as he enumerated, with deliberation, these certainties.

He was silent and thoughtful for some time. At last he said:

W.— "I confess your reasons seem to render it very certain that the law I read from Numbers is the same to which Jesus referred in his language to John. But there is one difficulty in the way of my believing that that is the law."

P.— "And what is that?"

W.— "The gospel history declares that Jesus was immersed."

P.— "That is an assumption. It does not say so."

W.— "In the first chapter of Mark, it says, 'In those days Jesus came from Nazareth of Galilee and was baptized by John in the Jordan. And when he came up out of the water, immediately he saw the heavens being torn open and the Spirit descending on him like a dove.'"[4]

P.— "In which statement do you find the immersion?"

W.— "It says he was baptized 'in Jordan,' and he 'came up out of the water.'"

P.— "Does it say that John put him down into or under the waters?"

W.— "No; but Jesus went down into the water, and came up out of it."

P.— "And did not John do the same?"

W.— "Well, yes."

P.— "And was he, too, immersed?"

W.— "No; but he did not go into the water to be immersed."

P.— "But your only evidence that Jesus was immersed, from circumstantial evidence, *is that he did just what John did.*"

W.— "If John did not immerse him, I do not know why he took him into the water."

P.— "To baptize him."

W.— "But the fact that he went into the water shows that he was immersed."

P.— "Must every one that goes *into* the water *go under it*? I have seen scores of men go into the water at the same time, to bathe, or

4 Mark 1:9.

wash, or cleanse themselves, and not one-fourth of them *go under it*, or *immerse* themselves. It has been my custom for many years to go into the water to bathe or wash; but only when a boy did I immerse myself, and *then* not as a mode of cleansing, but for amusement. For bathing I prefer shallow water, a running brook, though it were but a few inches in depth."

W.— "But if they went into the water, they were partly immersed."

P.— "Very true; but is this what you insist on as the immersion?"

W.— "No; but in performing a rite, I do not see why they would go into the water unless they would immerse."

P.— "And I do not see why they should immerse when they went into it."

W.— "Then why would they go into it?"

P.— "Not, very certainly, for absolute or literal cleansing [though if that had been the object, immersion need not have followed; and, if it had, it would have been an accidental circumstance]; but to use water in some way to represent cleansing. Now, laying aside all preconceived notions of immersion, is it reasonable to take it for granted that Jesus was immersed?"

W.— "I have always so taken it for granted. According to your own statement of its object, that is, to represent cleansing, it would certainly be accomplished by immersion, that is, to represent complete cleansing."

P.— "I fear that, too, is taken for granted."

W.— "I do not understand you. Laying aside your preconceived notions, will you not admit that immersion will better represent complete cleansing than simply applying a small quantity of water?"

P.— "The question is pointed and fair, but I will let God himself and Jesus answer it. I might ask you if it was not the purpose of

God, in the consecration of the Levites, to give a rite that would represent their complete cleansing? But for that purpose God was satisfied that a small quantity of water should be sprinkled upon them. Scores of such examples could be given from the Old Testament ablutions, or, as Paul, in Hebrews, calls them, baptisms. But I will refer you, for further answer to your question, to the language of Jesus, in the thirteenth chapter of John."

W.— "I do not recollect it. Will you state it?"

P.— "After the institution of the Supper, on the night of the betrayal, Jesus took a towel and wrapped himself. After that he poured water into a basin and began to wash his disciples' feet. When he came to Peter, Peter declined to submit to it. But Jesus said, 'If I do not wash you, you have no share with me.' Simon Peter said to him, 'Lord, not my feet only but also my hands and my head!' But the reply of Jesus was, 'he one who has bathed does not need to wash, except for his feet, *but is completely clean.'*[5] Does this answer your question?"

W.— "It would seem that it ought to be sufficient. But I do not see why they would go to the river and to where there was much water, if they did not immerse."

P.— "If you consider the facts, it would be strange if they had not gone to such places."

W.— "Why so?"

P.— "The history tells us that immense multitudes flocked to John, and were baptized by him. They regarded him as the forerunner of the long promised and now expected Messiah. 'Then Jerusalem and all Judea and all the region about the Jordan were going out to him, and they were baptized by him in the river Jordan, confessing their sins.'[6] Anticipating such crowds to

---

[5] John 13:8-10.
[6] Matthew 3:5-6.

attend on his ministry and to be baptized by him— and required by the nature of his mission and Old Testament prophecies to go into the wilderness— to what place should he go to find water, not only for baptizing but for the wants of the multitude and their animals?"

W.— "I suppose you think John did not immerse any of those who came to him?"

P.— "Not only do I suppose he did not, but that he would not have done so, had any requested it of him. It would fail to meet one great object of his baptism. Said he, 'I have baptized you with water, but he will baptize you with the Holy Spirit.'[7] He regarded his baptism as typical of that by the Spirit: and the Spirit descended on men; they were not dipped into it."

W.— "We are examining cases of the administration of the rite in the light of circumstantial evidence; what is there— of this kind— that warrants you in denying that it was by immersion?"

P.— "If I was to be tried for my life on circumstantial evidence half as clear, I would expect to be hung. John's ministry lasted about six months. From the passage already quoted, telling of the multitudes who came to him and were baptized by him, the number baptized, at a moderate estimate, was two or three hundred thousand, or an average of from one thousand to fifteen hundred per day."

W.— "But how could he baptize so many?"

P.— "Not at all, if the rite had been by immersion; but very easily as he performed the rite."

W.— "And how was that?"

P.— "The history does not inform us; but we are safe in concluding that it was like the baptism of the Old Testament economy.

---

[7] Mark 1:8.

Hebrews 9:19, will assist in answering your question. Will you please read it?"

W.— "'For when every commandment of the law had been declared by Moses to all the people, he took the blood of calves and goats, with water and scarlet wool and hyssop, and sprinkled both the book itself and all the people.'"

P.— "From the passage just read, and from many similar ones in the Old Testament, it is probable that John baptized by means of a hyssop branch, a shrub frequently used for that purpose in former times, and peculiarly adapted to such use. By such means he could have baptized many thousands in a day without extraordinary effort."

W.— "Then I suppose you think the three thousand were thus baptized in Jerusalem in the one day."

P.— "Very much in the same manner. The surrounding circumstances were somewhat different. There was no river in or near Jerusalem. The great mass of the Jews, and their leaders, all were the enemies of the Christians, and if the rite had been by immersion, there would have been two obstacles in the way:

"First, In finding any place for such wholesale immersion.

"Second, In being permitted to perform the rite in that way, had they found a place.

"Both these difficulties are fatal to the notion that it may have been by immersion. It would be difficult to find a city in the world, even among those that have rivers running near or through them, where, so promptly, with so little searching, and so little preparation, so many immersions could take place. It was nine o'clock when Peter began his sermon. How long he preached we are not informed. A portion of his sermon is given. In the 40th verse it is said, 'And with many other words he bore witness and continued to exhort them, saying, "Save yourselves from this crooked generation."' The whole account of the

82

baptism is given in the next verse; 'so those who received his word were baptized, and there were added that day about three thousand souls.' This would be a wonderful manner of disposing of a work of such magnitude as the immersion of a multitude in such a place as Jerusalem, and in so short a time. The account accords entirely with the Old Testament mode of administering the rite. According to the method given in Hebrews 9:19, two hours would have sufficed for procuring the water and baptizing the whole number by the apostle."

W.— "I confess that the immersion of those three thousand in one day has sometimes given me some trouble. But I have seen it stated that, from calculations, the thing is possible."

P.— "Did you ever make the calculation for yourself?"

W.— "No, sir, I never did."

P.— "Will you make it? I would like to see it."

W.— "Well, taking all the circumstances into the account, I suppose we may give them five hours."

P.— "That is a good allowance; but give them six."

W.— "There were twelve apostles, which would give, in all, seventy-two hours. This would assign about forty-two per hour to each apostle, or about ninety seconds for each immersion."

P.— "This supposes that the water was at hand; that everything was in readiness, and that there was no delay. How does it strike you?"

W.— "I was thinking that three minutes for each immersion would have been speedy work to perform the rite in a becoming manner. But then it would have required more than twelve hours. I do not know how the calculation was made."

P.— "Let us apply the rule to this case, and judging from circumstantial evidence, on which side does the evidence substantiate?"

W.— "To say nothing of the meaning of the word, or of the significance of the rite, I would have to admit that the theory of immersion finds very little sympathy from circumstantial evidence in those three thousand baptisms in one day."

P.— "The case of the three thousand is a digression. I scarcely know how we got astray to consider it. We were considering the baptism of Jesus and the multitudes that came to John. Returning to the latter, and applying the rule of circumstantial evidence, how does the case stand?"

W.— "To admit the numbers you say were baptized, of course it is absolutely certain they were not immersed. But I would not admit there were so many."

P.— "Very well; I think two hundred thousand would be a fair estimate. Shall we divide that number by two?"

W.— "That is still too high. Five would not be too large a divisor."

P.— "That would bring the number down to forty thousand. And now, to see how the matter would stand, let us divide it again by four, and we have ten thousand. Suppose, then that during his ministry of six months, he spent four days of each week in administering this rite. This would allow one hundred days, and give him an average of one hundred immersions for each day. At three minutes for each immersion, this would require him to stand in the water five hours per day. How close it appear when thus viewed?"

W.— "I scarcely know what to say."

P.— "Do you think flesh and blood could endure such labors?"

W.— "They would be exhausting."

P.— "It is almost certain that no man could continue such labors for half of one month. It is doubtful if he could endure it for four days; and to put the numbers at a fair estimate, we see the conclusive force of the circumstantial evidence. But to return to the case of Jesus, what verdict shall we record?"

W.— "I scarcely know. That was one of my strongest passages. If we decide according to the rule we adopted, and lay aside the idea of a burial, also the meaning of the word, and decide from circumstances alone, and in the light of the law he was to comply with, the case seems to be a hard one for me. I confess there is but little circumstantial evidence in the facts that point to immersion."

P.— "I thought we could dispose of these cases of the administration of the rite in one evening. But I see we cannot. You can meditate on those already considered, and, if convenient, return tomorrow evening."

W.— "*I have* another case of immersion I am anxious to know how you will dispose of. It is recorded in Acts 8:36-39. It says, 'And as they were going along the road they came to some water, and the eunuch said, "See, here is water! What prevents me from being baptized?" And he commanded the chariot to stop, and they both went down into the water, Philip and the eunuch, and he baptized him. And when they came up out of the water, the Spirit of the Lord carried Philip away, and the eunuch saw him no more, and went on his way rejoicing. '"

P.— "And this, you think, is a clear case of immersion?"

W.— "It has always appeared so to me."

P.— "In which statement does the immersion appear?"

W.— "In all the circumstances. They both went down into the water, and both came up out of the water."

P.— "If these circumstances prove immersion, then both were immersed; for precisely the same is said of the one that is said of the other. Is immersion any more apparent from this than from the similar statement in reference to the baptism of Jesus?"

W.— "No, it is the same. But taking all the circumstances into consideration, it seems most probable that the Eunuch was immersed."

P.— "But what circumstances?"

W.— "The meaning of the word and their going down into the water, etc."

P.— "Perhaps your meaning is this: taking it for granted that baptism means immersion, and can mean nothing else, then it seems, from these circumstances, that here was a case of immersion. You here advance what logicians call '*argumentum in circulo*,' arguing in a circle— a very common fallacy. Thus, in examining the word to find its meaning, we would say, 'It certainly means to immerse, because the circumstances so indicate.' Then, in examining the cases of its administration in the light of circumstantial evidence, you would say, 'The circumstances indicate immersion, because the word means to immerse.'"

W.— "But does it not seem most probable, in this case, that the rite was performed by immersion?"

P.— "On the contrary, everything opposes such a conclusion, except the assumption that in apostolic times they immersed."

W.— "What do you mean by everything?"

P.— "I mean all the circumstantial evidence.

"First, from our knowledge of the country. Gaza was some forty or fifty miles southwest from Jerusalem. From the account of the country given in Old Testament history, we learn that it was a ruggedly cratered region. This we learn from the fact that wells were dug to secure a supply of water for animals, and a well was regarded as a valuable possession, and often led to contention and strife. We have an account of such wells in connection with the history of Abraham and Lot. Also, when Abraham's servant went to secure a wife for Isaac, he stopped at a well, and Rebecca came out to draw water. In Exodus 2:16; 1 Samuel 9:11, and Jeremiah 7:3, and in many other places we learn the value of wells. From these facts, and our knowledge of the country at the present time, the circumstantial evidence is decidedly against the probability of their finding water that would suffice for immersion.

"Second, if we examine the passage, we can see that the Eunuch had some idea of baptism; he felt that it was his duty to be baptized. From this it would follow that Philip had given him some instruction on the subject. But the burden of his instructions, as we learn, was an exposition of the portion of Scripture he was reading. We infer, then, that the passage read must have contained some reference to baptism. Let us examine it. At the time he was accosted by Philip, he was reading the first part of the fifty-third chapter of Isaiah, as we learn from the quotation. He was then reading the first part of this chapter, and of course, had been reading for some time. The book of Isaiah was not then divided into chapters and verses. Now let us see if we can find anything in the passage that could have suggested the subject of baptism. Yes, in the immediate context, in what is now— in the divisions of the book— the last verse of the fifty-second chapter, we find, 'So shall He *sprinkle many nations.*'

"Here, then, water was spoken of, which accords with the narrative; 'And as they were going along the road they came to some water, and the eunuch said, "See, here is water! What prevents me from being baptized?'

"It is clear that Philip must have spoken to him of water; and the water must have been spoken of in the passage read by the eunuch; and we have found it: it had been read by the eunuch not two minutes before Philip addressed him. He had asked

Philip what the prophet meant by saying many nations should be *sprinkled*, and Philip explained to him the necessity of the Spirit's work: and how the water of baptism was the symbol of that cleansing, descending, or being sprinkled upon those who trust in Jesus.

"Third, From what has been stated, the natural conclusion is, the water to which they came was small in quantity. This is in harmony with the statement that both went into it. Wearing sandals, they could, without any inconvenience, descend into the shallow water, and Philip, taking water in his hand, sprinkled it upon the eunuch, in accordance with the passage he had read, and in accordance with the only scriptural mode of administering the rite.

"That such were the facts, we find additional evidence from the entire absence of any hint as to any preparation for immersion, or any arrangement for dry apparel afterwards. If it had been an immersion, we would expect some such circumstances mentioned, especially as the record informs us of a less important particular that 'he commanded the chariot to stop.'

"The narrative closes with the statement, 'when they came up out of the water, the Spirit of the Lord carried Philip away, and the eunuch saw him no more, and went on his way rejoicing. But Philip found himself at Azotus," from which we may suggest —

"First, Philip's departure was sudden.

"Second, It is not probable that, traveling on foot, he had a change of clothing.

"Third, It is equally improbable that he would go to Azotus, fifteen or twenty miles distant, in his dripping apparel."

W.— "All you have said is very plausible, but it is mere conjecture, and it is as easy to conjecture one thing as another. Is it proper to base an opinion on, or draw a conclusion from, such conjectures?"

P.— "You must remember, my dear sir, that we are now in search of probable or circumstantial evidence. In attempting to establish anything by such evidence, the only proper course is to frame hypotheses, and see if all the known facts harmonize with them.

"Your hypothesis is that the eunuch was immersed. The probabilities are all against it. My hypothesis is that a small quantity of water was applied to him, sprinkled upon him. All the circumstances favor it. How does the case appear to you?"

W.— "I confess I do not see the immersion as clearly as I once did."

P.— "Have you another case to suggest?"

W.— "None others suggest themselves to my mind."

P.— "Do you remember the baptism of Cornelius?"

W.— "Yes, sir, but I did not think it would throw any light on the question of mode."

P.— "Did you ever examine the narrative with the view to see if it does?"

W.— "No, sir, I cannot say that I did."

P.— "Let us look at it for a moment. It is found in the tenth chapter of Acts. At the conclusion of the narrative we are told, 'while Peter was still saying these things, the Holy Spirit fell on all who heard the Word. And the believers from among the circumcised who had come with Peter were amazed, because the gift of the Holy Spirit was poured out even on the Gentiles. For they were hearing them speaking in tongues and extolling God. Then Peter declared, "Can anyone withhold water for baptizing these people, who have received the Holy Spirit just as we have?" And he commanded them to be baptized in the name of Jesus

Christ. Then they asked him to remain for some days.'[1] I would like to ask you a few questions in reference to this narrative."

W.— "It will afford me pleasure to answer them to the best of my ability."

P.— "First, then, what suggested to Peter the propriety of baptizing Cornelius and his household?"

W.— "The account given says it was because they had received the Holy Spirit."

P.— "Please state what the narrative says as to the manner of their receiving the Holy Spirit."

W.— "It says the Holy Spirit fell on them. And again it speaks of Him as poured out on them."

P.— "The circumstance, then, that Peter saw the Holy Spirit fall on them, or poured out on them, suggested to him the propriety of baptizing them with water? Would it be proper, and in harmony with other passages, to express these facts in this way: 'When Peter saw that they were baptized with the Holy Spirit, then he saw that they should be baptized with water?'"

W.— "I see no objection to it."

P.— "Do these incidental facts suggest anything as to mode?"

W.— "I suppose they would to any one who believes in sprinkling."

P.— "Without any degree of violence, the passage, as we last gave it, admits a very suggestive variation. In this, for 'baptized," in the first clause, we will substitute the equivalent term found in the narrative, and change the latter clause to conform to it. It will then be 'When Peter saw that the Holy Spirit *fell on them*, then he saw that the water of baptism should *fall on them.*' But again, how does Peter present the question of their being baptized?"

---

[1] Acts 10:44-48.

W.— "By asking if any man can withhold water."

P.— "On the assertion that there was a place not very far distant where Peter intended to have them immersed, is the language used by him the most natural that suggests itself to your mind?"

W.— "I would have expected him to ask, 'Can any one withhold us to go to the water.'"

P.— "Then with which hypothesis does Peter's question best accord: That they were to go to the water, or that the water was to be brought to them?"

W.— "The form of his question agrees best with the latter assertion."

P.— "Now let us apply our rule of circumstantial evidence. To one wholly unprejudiced, ignorant of the contest about mode in baptism, but informed simply that the two modes are possible, to which of these do you think he would regard this narrative as pointing?"

W.— "Taken by itself the circumstances would seem to favor the application of water to them."

P.— "Do you recall another case of the administration of the rite?"

W.— "None of special interest."

P.— "Is not the baptism of Paul recorded?"

W.— "Since you mention it, I recollect that it is."

P.— "Will you please read the passage relating to his baptism? It is Acts 9:18."

W.— "'And immediately something like scales fell from his eyes, and he regained his sight. Then he rose and was baptized.'"

P.— "To my mind, the circumstantial evidence derived from this passage is peculiarly strong and in favor of our mode of baptism."

W.— "I never noticed anything striking in the account."

P.— "Are you aware of Paul's physical condition when Ananias went to him?"

W.— "In the ninth verse it stated that for three days he neither ate nor drank."

P.— "What is implied in the nineteenth verse?"

W.— "It says when he had received food he was strengthened."

P.— "Do not these facts indicate great physical prostration?"

W.— "They certainly do."

P.— "On the assertion that he was to be immersed, what would you regard as a fit time to attend to that duty?"

W.— "As soon as his strength would admit of it."

P.— "If the case had been left to you, would you have started with him on foot, or in some vehicle provided for the purpose, in search of a suitable place to immerse him while he was in such an enfeebled condition, before giving him any nourishment to strengthen him?"

W.— "Most certainly I would not."

P.— "And when was he baptized?"

W.— "The history does not inform us."

P.— "Please read the eighteenth and nineteenth verses."

W.— "'And immediately something like scales fell from his eyes, and he regained his sight. Then he rose and was baptized; and taking food, he was strengthened. For some days he was with the disciples at Damascus.' I see the force of your argument. He was baptized before he received food. It is certainly a remarkable circumstance."

P.– "If you will examine your Greek Testament, you will see some more very strong circumstantial evidence, that is to me decisive as to the mode of his baptism. The word translated 'rose,' is a participle, meaning 'rising,' or 'standing up.' He received sight immediately, and *rising* or *standing up*, he was baptized. And when he had received food he was strengthened. What think you now of the circumstantial evidence afforded by the baptism of Paul?"

W.– "I can readily understand how it would have great weight with those entertaining your views of baptism."

P.– "Do you think of another instance of the administration of the rite?"

W.– "I think all have been mentioned."

P.– "There are some instances with which you do not seem to be as familiar as with the baptism of Jesus and of the eunuch."

W.– "I have been accustomed to refer to them in arguing on the question of baptism. What case, not yet mentioned, is recorded?"

P.– "One of great interest; the baptism of the jailer at Philippi , and his household."

W.– "Since you mentioned it, I remember it. But I do not see that it throws any light on the question of mode. Its only statement is that he baptized him."

P.– "We are now in search of circumstantial evidence. I think a slight examination of the circumstances attending this baptism will show you that it is rich in this kind of evidence. It is recorded in the sixteenth chapter of Acts. Do you remember the general facts?"

W.–"I remember that Paul and Silas went to Philippi; and because of their preaching, and because of a miracle wrought by Paul, they were seized and cast into prison."

P.— "Do you remember any particular charge given to the jailer by the magistrates?"

W.— "I will see. Yes, in the twenty-third verse, it is said he was charged to keep them safely."

P.— "And how did he comply with this charge?"

W.— "He thrust them into the inner prison, and made their feet fast in the stocks."

P.— "What idea does this suggest as to the construction of the prison?"

W.— "I suppose it had an outer apartment for ordinary prisoners, and an inner apartment for keeping some more safely."

P.— "The history tells us there was an earthquake, and that all the doors were opened; and the jailer being awakened, and seeing the doors of the prison open, supposing the prisoners had escaped, was about to slay himself. Can you tell me when this occurred?"

W.— "It says it happened about midnight."

P.— "What did the jailer do when Paul cried to him, and assured him the prisoners were all there?"

W.— "He called for a light, and sprang up, and came trembling, and fell down before Paul and Silas, and brought them out, and said, 'Sirs, what must I do to be saved?'"[2]

P.— "Brought them 'out' of what, and into what?"

W.— "I suppose out of the inner prison, into which they had been thrust, into the outer apartment."

P.— "After Paul and Silas had answered his question— told him what he must do to be saved— what then took place? What did the jailer then do?"

---

[2] Acts 16:30.

W.— "He took them the same hour of the night and washed their stripes."

W.— "And was baptized, he and all his, straightway."

P.— "When did this baptism take place?"

W.— "It was between midnight and daylight; perhaps about two o'clock."

P.— "Where did the baptism take place?"

W.— "It does not tell us."

P.— "If by immersion, do you think it was in the prison?"

W.— "I never knew a jail to have such accommodations. They were not, in those days, as merciful to their prisoners as civilized nations now are. But there was a river near the city of Philippi ."

P.—"You do not think, then, that they were immersed inside of the jail?"

W.— "No; I think that is so highly improbable as to amount to a practical impossibility."

P.— "But you think they may have gone to that river?"

W.— "Yes, they must have gone there."

P.— "Who were baptized?"

W.— "The jailer and his family."

P.— "Did he have any children?"

W.— "It is not stated."

P.— "If there were but husband and wife, how, probably, would it have been stated?"

W.— "I suppose it would have been simply, 'the jailer and his wife.' The language implies that there were children."

P.— "And you think the jailer locked up the other prisoners; and that he, and his wife, and his children, accompanied by Paul and Silas, went down to the river at that midnight hour, and were there immersed, and then returned to the prison, and prepared a meal for the two preachers."

W.— "I do not see why they were so hasty in baptizing them, why they did not wait until daylight?"

P.— "Is it not an extraordinary— an unlooked for event— for Paul and Silas to take that man, and his wife, and his children, at that unreasonable hour, away to the river, and in the darkness of midnight, to immerse them, to say nothing of the jailer providing two suits of dry clothing. One for himself and one for one of the apostles?"

W.— "I confess it was remarkable."

P.— "In the light of circumstantial evidence, which theory of baptism has most to favor it in this case?"

W.— "You have made a strong case of it. I can see no room for immersion in it, only on the assumption that that is or was the only mode of baptism. I never thought that so strong a case could be made of it."

P.— "We have not seen its full strength yet. What did the magistrates do when it was daylight?"

W.— "They sent to the jailer to let those men go."

P.— "And did they go?"

W.— "No, Paul refused to go, or to leave the prison, until the magistrates would come and bring them out."

P.— "Do you think Paul and Silas were honest men?"

W.— "Why do you ask such a question?"

P.— "To get an answer, and thereby to make a point."

W.— "Of course they were honest."

P.— "Could they, as honest men, send the magistrates the word they did, refusing to go out of the walls of the prison until the magistrates would go and take them out; could they, as honest men, have thus spoken and acted, *if they had been outside of the prison during the night* without the knowledge or consent of the magistrates?"

W.— "I see the point of your argument and feel its force. I think we must regard it as certain that they did not leave the prison during the night."

P.— "It is not necessary to ask you which view of baptism this case most favors.

"We have now considered the subject according to agreement, confining ourselves to the Word of God alone.

I. "We endeavored to find the meaning of the word employed to designate the rite. We restricted our examination to its use in the Bible.

    A. "Because we wish to know how sacred writers understood and used the word.

    B. "Because a discussion of its classic use would be interminable; and, however decided, would be unsatisfactory.

"In ascertaining the meaning of the word, we pursued the plan that is pursued by all lexicographers in giving their definitions. We selected passages in which the circumstances attending the use of the word would throw light on its meaning. In that investigation we discovered two facts:

    A. "The word '*baptidzo*,' occurs nowhere in the Bible where the context indicates that its meaning is to immerse. Not a single passage can be pointed out.

"The word found in the fourth chapter of Daniel, and there translated 'wet,' i.e., moistened by dew, occurs several times in the New Testament, sometimes to indicate partial immersion. Thus, Luke 16:24, 'end Lazarus to dip the end of his finger, etc.; Matthew 26:23, 'He who has dipped his hand in the dish with me;' Revelation 19:13, 'He is clothed in a robe dipped in blood.' In the last quotation the meaning is very much the same as in Daniel. His garments became bloody in his conflicts with the enemy, by which the blood was applied to, or sprinkled upon the garment.

"If this word should be brought into the argument, and I do not see why it should not, then the '*baptidzo*,' leaves them without any Bible foundation for their use of the word.

B. "The other fact learned is that in several places the word is used in the sense of applying water to that which was baptized.

II. "We considered the significance of the rite; assumptions of immersionists would be destroyed by the passage in Daniel. To restrict ourselves to what it was intended to symbolize or commemorate. In this investigation we found:

A. "It was in no way connected with a burial.

    1. "Immersion would no better symbolize the disposition that was made of the dead body of Jesus than would sprinkling.

    2. "His burial had nothing to do with his work as our Redeemer. That work would have been as complete if the body of Jesus had not been buried at all.

    3. "That his resurrection, which immersionists associate with his burial, is abundantly commemorated by the Christian Sabbath.

4. "There is no passage in the Word of God that suggests that baptism was intended to have any connection with, or reference to, a burial.

B. "We found that baptism was intended to signify, or symbolize and commemorate, the work of the Holy Spirit. The water, and blood, and the Spirit agree in one.

C. "We found that in no case are we represented as immersed into the Holy Spirit. But on the other hand the Spirit is often spoken of as shed on us; as poured on us; as descending on us; as falling on us; from all of which but one conclusion can be drawn, and that is, in order to represent the work of the Spirit, *water must be applied to the individual.*

III. "We examined all the cases of its administration recorded that would throw any light on the question of mode.

"We examined the circumstances attending the baptism of the multitudes by John; also the baptism of Jesus; of the three thousand in one day; of the eunuch by Philip; of Cornelius by Peter; of Paul by Ananias; of the Philippian jailer and his household by Paul and Silas.

"We examined all these cases in the light of circumstantial evidence; and in every case we found the evidence conclusive against immersion, and in favor of the application of water to those baptized.

"These three methods of investigation are independent of each other. A conclusion reached by either method would suffice. But for the harmony and consistency of the sacred record, they ought to agree with each other. By each method the same conclusion is reached.

"Our method of inquiry must commend itself to you as the only one that is legitimate and satisfactory.

"I need not ask you to what conclusion you have come, as that is clearly indicated by your admissions. But I would make this suggestion: Before you make a final decision, go to the Rev. Mr. R. and ask him to go over the whole subject with you as I have. First, let him give you the meaning of the word. He will tell you it means to immerse, and nothing else. Ask him for proof; but confine him to the *Bible*, for the reasons I have already mentioned.

"Ask him in reference to the significance of the rite, and let him give his authority for the assumption that it has any reference to a burial. When he quotes the sixth chapter of Romans, ask him for a detailed interpretation of the passage.

"Let him examine all the cases of the administration of the rite in the light of circumstantial evidence. In the baptism of Jesus ask him to explain, 'thus it is fitting for us to fulfill all righteousness.'[3]

"In the whole discussion, let him confine himself to the Bible, and let Pædobaptist concessions alone. Tell him that such *ad hominem* arguments do not apply to you.

"After such investigation let your decision be made independently of what I have said, or what he may say— guided only by your perception of the truth, with the Bible as your only authority.

"I would like to have you return one more evening, as there is a general view of the subject I would like to present, which, taken in connection with what has been said, will assist in coming to a clear and full understanding of the subject."

---

[3] Matthew 3:15.

SEVENTH EVENING: SIMPLICITY OF BAPTISM

W.— "On the last night I was here I did not retire to bed until after midnight, and then I sought sleep in vain. I heard the clock strike one, two, three and four, but I could not dismiss the subject of baptism from my mind. All our interviews passed in review before me. I was determined not to believe that the views I had entertained on the subject of baptism are erroneous. I reconsidered the meaning of the word from its use in the Bible; but those passages you quoted seemed to have inscribed beneath them, and underscored, *no immersion here.*

"I went to the significance of the rite. I said it must commemorate a burial. But I labored in vain to find a shadow of a foundation for such a view. The more I thought of it, the more I was amazed that I ever could, in the light of the New Testament, fail to see that baptism can refer to anything but the cleansing by the Spirit. The burial theory was so completely buried that I could find no trace of it.

"I then appealed to the recorded instances of its administration. The old familiar cases of the baptism of Jesus by John, and of the eunuch by Philip, seemed strange to me. The old landmarks had been removed.

"I looked to see John the Baptist, waist deep in water, immersing the multitudes that came to him. I tried to persuade him to occupy that position; but he cast on me a look of astonishment and plea, as if to say, 'Am I a God, that I could thus stand and immerse these thousands that come to me for baptism!' and shod with sandals—standing in the brink of Jordan with hyssop branch in hand— he called to them around him to repent, and be baptized for the remission of their sins: and as they sometimes several in a group, the hyssop branch was dipped in the Jordan, and with one motion of his hand the work was done; the water in gentle spray, descended upon them.

"I thought of the baptism of Cornelius, and of Paul and the Philippian jailer and his household; but nothing but images of the descent of water on them filled my vision.

"The next evening I went to see Mr. R. He had heard of my frequent interviews with you, and soon inquired how I was getting along on the subject of baptism.

"I told him I was in great trouble. He wanted to know the nature of my troubles. I told him you had presented the subject in a light entirely new to me, and that I was wholly unable to meet your arguments.

"I then asked him if he would go over the whole subject with me as you have done. His reply was that he would; but that one evening would be sufficient. He said he could bring any number of Greek lexicons that: would testify that the word means to immerse.

"He suggested that the best plan was for me to read a work on the subject by a learned Pædobaptist: Prof. Stuart on Baptism. He assured me that after reading the concessions of this able writer I would he satisfied.

"I told him I cared nothing about the concessions of any man, unless all on his side of the question would assent to them. What I was after was Bible truth.

"He said he did not see how the question could be considered from an exclusively Bible standing point. This seemed strange after all I had heard them say on the subject, affirming that they alone had the Bible on their side."

P.— "I am glad you visited Mr. R., but am sorry he did not consent to a consideration of the subject as you proposed.

"It would give him pleasure to refer you to a few Greek lexicons as authority for his view on the classic meaning of the word.

"If you desire such a consideration of the subject, outside of the Bible, I would refer you a work by Dr. Dale, on the classic use of the word— a work of 400 or 500 pages— wherein he shows, in a most unanswerable manner by innumerable quotations from classic Greek writers, that the word did not mean to immerse.

"As to the concessions of Prof. Stuart, they are utterly worthless, as you very properly suggested to Mr. R., unless in a controversy with those who would make the same concessions.

"If his concessions are of a character to convince you they ought to have convinced the professor himself. The very fact that he was not convinced, shows one of three things:

1. "That the concessions are not as important and convincing as Baptists pretend; or—

2. "That the professor was so ignorant or stupid, or both, that he could not draw a legitimate conclusion from them; or—

3. "That he was very dishonest in holding one theory and practicing another. Thus you see in any case it would be very stupid in any one to allow himself to be influenced by them.

"This work by Stuart was republished by Graves, Marks & Co., a Baptist house in Nashville, Tennessee; and to show you how Stuart's friends regarded his concessions, let me read to you an extract from a commendatory notice of the work: it is by G. S. Baker, formerly editor of the Christian Index, Ga. After speaking of the obligations under which the Baptist denomination is to Graves, Marks & Co., for republishing the work, he says, 'Nearly twenty years ago I urged upon brothers to endeavor to have an edition of it removed from circulation by Baptists, but was informed that it could not be done, as the author's brothers in the church were very much displeased with him for its publication, and were buying up all the copies they could find in order to suppress it.'

"This writer concedes that Stuart stood almost alone in his concessions; his friends were displeased with him for making and publishing them; they would not agree to them. Whence, then, their value in an argumentative point of view?

"Why, then, it might be asked, did the Baptists republish such a work for circulation among their adherents?

"The answer is easily given. Because it would tickle and establish those already convinced, and influence the ignorant and unthinking; and especially because they have nothing better to put forth in favor of their assumptions.

"But let me ask, how does the matter stand with you now?"

W.— "I do not see that immersion can claim any authority or warrant from the Word of God."

P.— "The subject I intended to introduce this evening has, to my mind, great force independently of all other considerations. But, perhaps, it will not be necessary to call your attention to these facts, as you are already satisfied."

W.— "I am interested in the subject, and will be glad to hear anything you have to say on it."

P.— "I proposed to consider the question from what philosophers call an *a priori*[1] standpoint."

W.— "By which you mean what we might have expected or anticipated beforehand from the nature of things."

P.— "Yes, sir; what we might have anticipated from the nature of the New Testament dispensation, as distinguished from the Old."

W.— "I do not believe that I understand how a conclusion can be drawn from such premises."

P.— "Can you tell me what was the nature of the service required of those under the Old Testament dispensation?"

W.— "I know that the duties imposed were often burdensome. They had a multitude of rites, various ablutions and sacrifices to offer, which required great self-denial and labor on the part of the worshipers."

P.— "And what is the peculiarity of the New Testament dispensation in this respect?"

W.— "Very different. It is remarkable for the fewness of its rites, and the simplicity of its service."

P.— "The difference between the two dispensations is very marked. We may take, as a fair example, the Feast of the Passover in the Old, and that which takes its place in the New the Lord's Supper. These will fairly represent the two dispensations in the peculiarities mentioned. What can you remember of the Passover as celebrated by the Jews before Christ came?"

W.— "I recollect it lasted seven days. All leaven was to be carefully removed from their dwellings; and a lamb was to be provided for

---

[1] A *priori* refers to that which can be verified apart from experience; in other words, that conclusion which can be realized deductively.

each household, which was to be slain, roasted, and eaten during the night."

P.— "And what can you say of that which takes its place in the New Testament dispensation?"

W.— "The Lord's Supper is in great contrast with it. It is remarkable for its simplicity."

P.— "The whole service of Judaism stands in as marked contrast with the service as instituted by Christ and his apostles. What was the particular rite, under the Old Testament, by which a man became, outwardly, a Jew?"

W.— "It was circumcision."

P.— "Was it remarkable for its simplicity?"

W.— "By no means. I think it agreed very well with the whole ceremonial service of that economy."

P.— "That is the rite by which we become or are recognized as Christians?"

W.— "The rite which we are now considering; and I begin to see the point and force of your argument."

P.— "How do circumcision and immersion compare in point of simplicity?"

W.— "It would be difficult to see any great difference in this respect. On many accounts I think the odds are in favor of circumcision."

P.— "But, reasoning from analogy, from the greater simplicity of the New Testament service in all things else, what would we have anticipated or expected in reference to the rite that was to take the place of circumcision?"

W.— "Most certainly that it would correspond with all other changes in its decidedly superior simplicity."

P.— "Again, I would ask you how does immersion strike you as a rite in the New Testament Church?"

W.— "I fully appreciate the force of the argument. I am surprised that it never suggested itself to my mind before. The church is called Christ's body; and immersion, as a rite in the New Testament Church, so remarkable for the simplicity of its service, seems like a huge, useless, and abnormal growth on the body of Christ, destroying its proportions and marring its beauty, and renders deformed what would otherwise have been symmetrical. It is like a great fifth wheel to a wagon. It does not fit; it does not work. I scarcely know how to illustrate it; but immersion seems to be a foreign element, out of its latitude— wholly out of place. It is like a cog wheel taken from the gearing of a saw-mill and attached to a family sewing machine."

P.— "I am glad you appreciate the force of this *a priori* argument. It was this that first led me to suspect the claims of immersionists, and to examine the Word of God in reference to baptism."

"When I was about the age at which you received the nickname 'William the Baptist,' my zeal for immersion was not much below yours at that age. At a revival of religion in Salem, Ohio, during the winter of 184-, about seventy persons united with the Baptist Church. Among the converts was my oldest sister, about eighteen years of age. The weather was intensely cold, and the ice on the pond about twelve inches thick. The pond in which they were immersed was about one mile distant. I went to the 'baptizing,' as they called it, to see my sister immersed. A large opening was made in the ice, and there, under such circumstances, was the rite administered. It made a deep impression on my mind. I thought each one deserved great credit to discharge such a duty; and I think such a spirit of self-righteousness is one of the strong pillars of its support.

"Although I have not since then seen the hymn sung on the occasion, yet I have a distinct recollection of one of the stanzas. It ran thus:

"'Christians, if your hearts are warm,
Ice and snow can do no harm;
If by Jesus you are prized,
Arise, believe, and be baptized.'[2]

"Such things satisfied my youthful mind at the time.

"Subsequently I knew of occasions where they had to go eight or ten miles to perform the rite.

"On one occasion, when about twenty were to be immersed, a small pond was made for the purpose by building a dam across a small stream of water. Before half a dozen had been immersed, the entrance became very miry, and the water decidedly muddy, and soon it became difficult to determine which predominated, the water or the mud.

"In some localities, and in some circumstances, as in the case of the sick, it is a physical impossibility to perform the rite by immersion.

"From such facts I was early led to wonder why a rite so Mosaic or Pharisaic in its nature, should mar the general simplicity of the church under the New Testament dispensation. This led me to examine the subject in the light of God's Word, and thus I soon found that immersion finds no warrant in the Word of God.

"As a mode of baptism it is unscriptural, failing in a very important particular to do that for which baptism was instituted;

---

[2] This is the first stanza of a hymn entitled, "Christians, If Your Hearts Are Warm" written by John Leland, a Baptist pastor who lived from 1754 to 1841; this particular hymn was published sometime after 1809, according to *Baptist Hymn Writers and Their Hymns* by Henry Sweetser Burrage (Portland, Maine: Brown, Thurston & Company, 1858), pp. 229-232.

that is, to symbolize the granting of the Holy Spirit, which can be accomplished only by the *application of water* to the individual."

William Unites With the Church, But Does Not Believe in Infant Baptism

About two weeks after our last interview was the time for our quarterly communion. Among those who presented themselves for membership was William. Happy and contented, he sat with his wife to celebrate the dying love of Jesus, whose blood cleanses from all sin; the application of whose blood had that morning been symbolized by the sprinkling of the purifying element on him. A few weeks afterwards, in a visit to the parsonage, he said he had been studying the principles of the Presbyterian Church, and expressed his decided approbation of "most of its doctrines and usages." One thing he mentioned with which he was pleased, namely: that those seeking membership were not expected or required to subscribe to all its doctrines. This, he continued, was fortunate for him, as he could not believe in infant baptism. He was glad that all are allowed to have their own views on this subject, and to present their children for baptism if they feel inclined, or as he thought was best— to let their children grow to a mature age and decide this matter for themselves.

PASTOR.— "What you say on this subject— liberty— is in part true; but as you state it, is liable to misunderstanding. In receiving members we do not ask them if they give assent to all our doctrines as set forth in our Confession of Faith and Catechisms. Officers only, at their installation, are required to give their assent to these. But it is expected that all persons, in seeking union with us, do agree with us on all the leading and important doctrines of our church. One point, mentioned by you, I deem of the greatest importance, and think some church sessions are culpable in allowing it to be ignored and neglected. I speak of the duty of Christian parents, members of our church, in dedicating their children to God in baptism."

W.— "You astonish me. I thought it was definitely understood that this matter was left entirely with the parents, and that church sessions had no business even to inquire into the reasons why any did not present their children. I have known many Presbyterians who did not believe in infant baptism, and did not have their children baptized, and I never heard of any being disciplined for such neglect. I knew an elder in the church who did not believe in it, and never presented any of his children for baptism, though he had several of them."

P.— "I expect you are mistaken in your last statement. It would be a remarkable fact if true; because, at his installation, in the presence of God and the congregation, he solemnly affirmed that he received, as in accordance with the Word of God, all the doctrines found in our standards. As to your statement about others— I am sorry to say I suppose it is true. At least some are not in accord with us, and neglect the performance of this duty. And, as I before remarked, I think sessions are culpable in quietly overlooking such omissions of duty."

W.— "Would you be in favor of disciplining an individual for not doing what he conscientiously thought he ought not to do?"

P.— "Not exactly in that form; rather admonishing him for not enjoying a privilege, and discharging a duty so clearly enjoined in the Word of God."

W.— "But suppose he cannot see it in the light of a privilege and duty?"

P.— "Then admonish him to search the Scriptures, and learn his duty."

W.— "I am entirely satisfied on the question of the mode of baptism; but infant baptism I regard as a relic of popery, and without any divine warrant. You had a difficult task to show me that immersion is not scriptural baptism. But to convince me that it is my duty to have my unconscious babies baptized, would be far more difficult."

P.— "I was not conscious of any great difficulty in the former task. I simply called your attention to a few facts in the Word of God. Allow me to say that the great secret of your former prejudice against infant baptism, and the reason of your inability, until now, to see the truth in reference to it was that your egregious errors on the question of mode cast such a shadow over it as to obscure and darken it beyond the possibility of recognition. While it is true that some receive both immersion and infant baptism, yet they are so repugnant to each other that it is difficult to keep them together. When about to immerse an adult, the person officiating can prevent bad consequences by whispering, 'hold your breath while under the water;' but such admonitions would be lost on a baby, and very unpleasant consequences would attend their immersion. Since your errors on the question of mode have been rectified, it will be an easy task to point out a few passages in the Word of God, where this duty is enjoined, and just as easy for you to see the truth."

W.— "Candor compels me to assure you that you are mistaken. I think the language found in the closing part of the book of

Revelation applies to the whole Word of God, especially to the ordinances of his house. 'I warn everyone who hears the words of the prophecy of this book: if anyone adds to them, God will add to him the plagues described in this book.'[1] I would not be satisfied with anything short of a positive command, a 'Thus Says The LORD;' and I know that no such authority is found in the Bible for infant baptism, for I have read it from Matthew to Revelation."

P.— "In all this, except your last statement, I agree with you. But you did not finish the quotation."

W.— "I gave all that I intended, or that I thought was appropriate."

P.— "That, as I shall show you, is the misfortune of all immersionists. Please quote the balance of the passage, as I shall call your attention to it at the proper time."

W.— "'I warn everyone who hears the words of the prophecy of this book: if anyone adds to them, God will add to him the plagues described in this book, and if anyone takes away from the words of the book of this prophecy, God will take away his share in the tree of life and in the holy city, which are described in this book.'"[2]

P.— "I wish you to bear in mind both these statements. One, you see, is attended with as serious consequences as the other. Immersionists charge us with 'adding to;' we confidently charge them with 'taking from.'"

W.— "But the point I make is a very simple one, and easily disposed of. It is this: In all religious ordinances and institutions, and in all duties that bind the conscience, there must be a positive command. The Church of Rome claims power to bind the conscience where the Bible has not done so. It claims the power to add to the ordinances of the House of

---

[1] Revelation 22:18
[2] Revelation 22:18-19

God. The Church, I maintain, has no such power. There must be a positive command, or we 'add to.'"

P.— "Would not legitimate, logical necessary inference be equivalent to a positive command, and be satisfactory to you?"

W.— "Inference is good in its place. But in such a case it will not meet the requirements of a positive command."

P.— "I propose to show you two facts, which now you would not acknowledge, but of the truth of which I intend to convince you: First, all Anti-pædobaptists take inference for a positive command in reference to the ordinances or institutions of religion. Second, we have a positive command, a 'Thus Says The LORD,' for dedicating our children to God, as our custom is."

W.— "I am afraid you have spoken hastily, and will find it very difficult to verify your statement."

P.— "Would you not admit that the church, in its collective capacity, in a general council, by unanimous consent, could change the day to be observed as the Christian Sabbath?"

W.— "No, sir, not by the consent of the whole church."

P.— "I agree with you. Would inference do for such a change?"

W.— "It must be a clear command."

P.— "On what authority has the change been made from the first day of the week to the last?"

W.— "I do not remember; but I presume the authority is positive and plain."

P.— "I will give it to you, as you are not familiar with it. Three or four passages will be enough to show you the nature of the authority, John 20:19: 'On the evening of that day, the first day of the week, the doors being locked where the disciples were for fear of the Jews, Jesus came and stood among them...' And verse 26: 'Eight days later, his disciples were inside again...' 1

117

Corinthians 16:2: 'On the first day of every week, each of you is to put something aside and store it up...' Do you see any positive command for the change of any of these passages?"

W.— "Nothing that has the appearance of such."

P.— "Yet it is from such passages, taken in connection with the fact that the Lord Jesus arose from the dead on the first day of the week, and from the fact that the early Christians celebrated the first day of the week as the Sabbath— it is from such passages that we get our warrant for the change. Is there, I repeat, a positive command or is it mere inference?"

W.— "Is there no better authority for the change?"

P.— "No better can be found."

W.— "Then it is certainly mere inference."

P.— "Have immersionists, who make such demands for a 'Thus Says The LORD,' for our warrant for infant baptism, and who will not listen to arguments from inference, any authority to observe the first day of the week as the Christian Sabbath?"

W.— "It is very certain that they must be satisfied with clear inference, or change back to Saturday."

P.— "Their stereotyped demand is a 'Thus Says The LORD;' 'a positive command' or 'no mere inference,' for any of the ordinances or institutions of religion. The plain, positive command, as given in the Scriptures, is: 'Remember the seventh day to keep it holy to the Lord.'[3] No positive command: no 'Thus Says The LORD,' can be pointed out for the change to the first day of the week. Then, consistency demands of them, as you say, to go back to the seventh day, or, like honest men, admit that we have sufficient authority for such a change in inferential arguments drawn from such passages as we have quoted, and

[3] Exodus 20:8-11; it is the last two verses of the passage that define the "Sabbath" day as the seventh day.

118

cease their repetition of a 'Thus Says The LORD' for everything pertaining to infant baptism."

W.– "Then your argument in favor of infant baptism is inferential, I suppose? Is it as clear as that in favor of the change of the Sabbath?"

P.– "I wish to impress it on your mind that the argument in favor of infant baptism, in its essential parts, is not at all inferential. It is in the form of a 'positive command,' a 'Thus Says The LORD.' In some of its aspects it is inferential; but in these cases the inference is very much clearer than that which satisfied immersionists in regard to the change of the Sabbath."

W.– "It is news to me that you can give a positive command, a 'Thus Says The LORD.' Do this and I am satisfied."

P.– "You are a lawyer by profession, and are thus specially qualified to appreciate the force of the argument. Will you tell me what is the nature, and, in point of time, the extent of the binding obligation of a law that has, in due form, been enacted?"

W.– "A law is binding from the time it is enacted by the proper authority until its obligation ceases by limitation, or until it is in due form repealed."

P.– "Can you tell me how this principle applies to the divine law?"

W.– "The Savior himself answers your question in his Sermon on the Mount. He says, 'Do not think that I have come to abolish the Law or the Prophets; I have not come to abolish them but to fulfill them. For truly, I say to you, until heaven and earth pass away, not an iota, not a dot, will pass from the Law until all is accomplished.'"[4]

P.– "Can you tell me to what law he refers in that statement?"

---

[4] Matthew 5:17-18.

W.– "Do you refer to the distinction between the ceremonial and moral law?"

P.– "Yes, sir."

W.– "I suppose he refers to both. The statement is applicable to both."

P.– "What does he mean by saying 'not an iota, not a dot, will pass from the Law?'"

W.– "He means that it shall not, in the least degree, be abrogated, nullified, or cease to be binding."

P.– "And what does he mean by the expression, 'until all is accomplished?'"

W.– "Until the end for which the law was enacted has been fully met and accomplished."

P.– "When thus fulfilled, does its obligation cease?"

W.– "It does then, and not until then."

P.– "Can you give me an example of such fulfillment from which the obligation to obey ceases, or the law ceases to be binding."

W.– "The law requiring sacrificial rites found its fulfillment in Christ. It was enacted that the Jews should bring their victims, and, in the manner prescribed, offer them in sacrifice to God. All these bloody sacrifices typified Christ, who would, in the fullness of time, offer himself a sacrifice to God. Since they typified him as the Lamb of God, they were fulfilled when he offered himself, and when his own blood was shed for us. Being fulfilled, such laws are no longer binding. Their object and end were fully met."

P.– "Your knowledge is accurate, and your views on this question are very correct. An interesting and instructive example is found in connection with an apartment of the temple. The part called the holy of holies was separated from the holy place by a veil.

120

Into that sacred enclosure no one could go, nor even look, save the high priest, and he but once a year, on the great day of atonement. In Hebrews we are informed that such a law was enacted to show us 'the way into the holy places is not yet opened as long as the first section is still standing.'[5] The apostle then shows us how all this pointed to Jesus, and typified his work. And when Christ was 'offered once to bear the sins of many,'[6] the writer says, 'since we have confidence to enter the holy places by the blood of Jesus, by the new and living way that he opened for us through the curtain, that is, through his flesh...'[7] In this he teaches us that the veil separating the holy place from the holy of holies, was typical of Christ and his work. Of course, then, the law requiring it was fulfilled when he performed the work typified, that is, when he entered into the holy placed not made with hands, that is, into heaven itself. What further need was there, then, of that holy of holies, and of the veil enclosing it? Therefore, in illustration of the principle we are considering, we are told that when Jesus cried with a loud voice, and gave up the Spirit, 'the curtain of the temple was torn in two, from top to bottom.'"[8]

W.— "All that is very clear, interesting and instructive; but I do not see how it bears on the subject we are considering."

P.— "We are preparing the way for 'a positive command,' a 'Thus Says The LORD.' Will you turn to Genesis 17:9-10, and read?"

W.— "'And God said to Abraham, "As for you, you shall keep my covenant, you and your offspring after you throughout their generations. This is my covenant, which you shall keep, between me and you and your offspring after you: Every male among you shall be circumcised."'"

---

[5] Hebrews 9:8.
[6] Hebrews 9:28.
[7] Hebrews 10:19-20.
[8] Matthew 27:51; cf. Mark 15:38.

P.— "Here we have a law, enacted by God himself. It is a positive command; a 'Thus Says The LORD.' And now comes the question, How long was this law to be binding?"

W.— "I suppose the law was peculiar to the Mosaic dispensation, and ceased with it."

P.— "On what principle?"

W.— "It is declared to be a covenant between Abraham and his seed. The Jews were his seed, and, therefore, it ceased with them."

P.— "Will you read Galatians 3:7?"

W.— "'Know then that it is those of faith who are the sons of Abraham.'"

P.— "Also the 29th verse."

W.— "'And if you are Christ's, then you are Abraham's offspring, heirs according to promise.'"

P.— "The covenant which God made with Abraham, as we shall see, was the covenant of grace, that he and his seed should be saved by faith. The passages quoted show clearly who are the seed of Abraham, as the term is used in the covenant. The Scriptures declare that it was not simply those who descended from Abraham; for many of his descendants were not included in this covenant."

W.— "But did not the whole ceremonial law cease to be binding when Christ came?"

P.— "On what principle, according to the text you quoted from the Sermon on the Mount, did they cease?"

W.— "In that Christ fulfilled them."

P.— "If it be true that Christ fulfilled the law we are now considering, then it is no longer binding. We have now reached a point in the discussion which immersionists ignore; a point where it is necessary for us to change sides. Up to this point the burden of proof has, very properly, fallen on me; now it falls to you. You stated what everyone will admit, that the law is of binding obligation until it is fulfilled, or until it is repealed. We have found a law, of divine enactment, requiring the seal of the covenant to be applied to children. Our work is done; yours, at this point, begins. It falls on you to show that the law is no longer binding."

W.— "I now see how you have been leading me. The point you make is new to me, and perfectly legitimate. I can readily understand how it strikes you as very strong. But I think I can convince you that it has ceased to be binding."

P.— "And failing to do so, what follows?"

W.— "Then, of course, the law is as binding as when first given to Abraham. In the first place, I affirm that this law ceased with all the other ceremonial laws of that dispensation."

P.— "This is mere assumption. I demand a 'Thus Says The LORD.'"

W.— "On the same principle you might say that many of the ceremonial laws are yet binding, because we cannot point to a 'Thus Says The LORD;' showing that they have been repealed."

P.— "Our demand is reasonable, and a necessity. You yourself have laid down the principle that a law is binding until fulfilled or repealed. We affirm that all the laws of the Old Testament are binding that have not ceased to be so in some of the methods enumerated by you. The truth is, most of the ceremonial laws were typical of Christ and his work, and were fulfilled by him, and therefore ceased. The law requiring us to observe the Sabbath was not typical of Christ nor his work, and was not fulfilled by him, therefore it is still binding. The law requiring Abraham and his seed after him to apply the seal of the covenant of grace to their infant children was not typical of Christ nor his work, and was not fulfilled by Christ. Thus, you

123

see, it is an assumption to say that this law ceased when such laws as those requiring sacrificial rites came to an end."

W.— "I see and appreciate the distinction you make. I remember the text, 'until heaven and earth pass away, not an iota, not a dot, will pass from the Law until all is accomplished.'[9] I acknowledge that this law was not fulfilled in Christ, nor by his work. But I will change the form of my argument. The law specifies that the children should be circumcised. Circumcision, as you will acknowledge, has ceased by divine authority; and therefore, in the very nature of the case, the law has ceased to be binding."

P.— "I am glad you are ready to acknowledge an error when it is made plain to you. But, giving up one assumption, you have fled to another. You now say that a thing is so in the very nature of the case. But I say that is an assumption. I affirm that the law requiring circumcision has not, in any proper sense of the word, ceased to be binding. Here I demand the proof, and will be satisfied with nothing but a 'Thus Says The LORD.'"

W.— "But the rite of circumcision has ceased. Do you deny that it has ceased by divine authority?"

P.— "I acknowledge that it has ceased, and that too by divine authority. But I called upon you to show me that authority."

W.— "I cannot, only that it ceased after the establishment of the New Testament Church. Can you give the authority or the reason of its cessation?"

P.— "I can."

W.— "Will you do it?"

P.— "The task belongs to immersionists, or the opposers of infant baptism, but they cannot do it. They propose to 'take from' the Word of God on mere assumption. Circumcision ceased in very

---

[9] Matthew 5:18.

much the same manner as did the feast of the Passover, by what may be called substitution. The law we are now considering is to be regarded in a two-fold aspect: First, and most important, requiring parents to consecrate their children to God; to have the seal of the covenant applied to them. Second, requiring circumcision, it being at that time the seal.

"It would indeed be a strange view to take of the law, to suppose that it required circumcision for the sake of circumcision. The essential part was the consecration or the application of the seal. The rite, which was then the seal, has ceased only by giving place to another of the same kind, or for the same purpose. The law requiring the consecration of children to God, or the application of the seal of the covenant to them, stands unfulfilled and un-repealed."

W.— "On what authority do you affirm that circumcision has ceased by giving place to another rite of the same kind, and for the same purpose? I suppose you mean that baptism has taken its place?"

P.— "It certainly has; and the proof is very clear. Firstly, they have the same object. Circumcision was the rite of initiation into the church under the Old Testament dispensation. It was by this rite that men became Jews. Baptism is the rite of initiation into the church under the New Testament dispensation. It is by this rite that we become or are recognized as Christians. Secondly, their significance is the same. Circumcision was intended to signify purity of heart. A few passages will make this evident. Deuteronomy 10:16, 'Circumcise therefore the foreskin of your heart, and be no longer stubborn.' Deuteronomy 30:5, 'And the LORD your God will bring you into the land that your fathers possessed, that you may possess it.' Jeremiah 4:4, 'Circumcise yourselves to the LORD; remove the foreskin of your hearts, O men of Judah and inhabitants of Jerusalem.' Romans 2:28-29, 'For no one is a Jew who is merely one outwardly, nor is circumcision outward and physical. But a Jew is one inwardly, and circumcision is a matter of the heart, by the Spirit, not by the letter. His praise is not from man but from God.' Baptism, as you well know, signifies the same thing. As John says, 'For there are three that testify: the Spirit and the water and the blood; and these three agree.'[10] The two former typify, and the last accomplishes, our cleansing. Thirdly, each sustains the same relation to the covenant of grace, that is, a seal to it."

W.— "The Jews occupied a peculiar position. They present themselves to us in the two-fold aspect of a state and a church. Was not circumcision, so to speak, a national badge; or was not circumcision intended to confer citizenship rather than church membership?"

P.— "This is an old objection; and the enemies of infant baptism show the poverty of their cause when they seek to evade the force of the truth by such expedients. It is true they were both a nation and a church, but it is also true that these two formed but one theocracy. There were not two governments. To belong to the nation was to belong to the church, and vice versa."

W.— "But did not circumcision belong to or pertain more to citizenship in the state than to membership in the church?"

P.— "What I have said as to the significance of the rite ought to be a sufficient answer to this question. But I will cite another authority to show you how exceedingly erroneous is such a view. When I told you that circumcision was the seal of the covenant of grace, I expected you to ask my authority for such a statement: but as you did not, I will anticipate such a demand, as my warrant for that statement will show you that circumcision had special reference to the church, as distinguished from the nation. Will you read Romans 4:11, the first part of the verse?"

---

[10] 1 John 5:7-8.

W.— "'He received the sign of circumcision as a seal of the righteousness that he had by faith while he was still uncircumcised.'"

P.— "To whom does the apostle here refer?"

W.— "To Abraham."

P.— "What is a seal?"

W.— "It is something applied to an agreement or covenant to establish or confirm it."

P.— "Of what was circumcision given as a seal?"

W.— "Of righteousness."

P.— "And what does this mean?"

W.— "'A seal of righteousness' means a confirmation of the fact that he was righteous."

P.— "And how did the righteousness come; or how did he get it?"

W.— "'A seal of the righteousness of faith,' that is, that his faith secured the righteousness."

P.— "We are taught that Abraham was justified by faith; that God regarded and treated him as righteous because of his faith; and in confirmation of the fact that he would so regard him, he gave him circumcision as a seal. We are here very clearly taught the object of circumcision at its institution; as it was given to Abraham, it was a 'seal of righteousness which is by faith, a seal of the covenant of grace.'[11] Does this language of Paul sufficiently answer your question?"

W.— "Yes, sir; I never saw circumcision in that light before. According to Paul's statement it is evident that, at the time of its institution, it had exclusive reference to the church, or, as you

---

[11] See Romans 4:11.

said, it was the seal of the covenant of grace. In its object and significance, it seems to have been identical with baptism."

P.— "The law requiring children to be consecrated to God has not been repealed; the rite by which the consecration was accomplished has ceased; but another rite, for the same object, and with the same significance, but simpler in its nature, is found in the New Testament Church. Is it not a necessity that we conclude that the one takes the place of the other?"

W.— "It would seem to be so. But there is a serious difficulty in the way, and that is, only male children were circumcised; and if one takes the place of the other, then only male children should be baptized. But you baptize children of both sexes."

P.— "The fact that baptism takes the place of circumcision is, of itself, a sufficient answer to this objection. But I will say further in answer to it:

1. "The seal of the covenant was, in its very nature, applicable only to males.

2. "It was not applied to females of any age; and therefore women, individually or personally, were not members of the church. They were regarded as represented by the males.

3. "In the New Testament Church, with a change of seal, a seal applicable to them, we find it was applied to them, as we learn from the case of Lydia.[12]

4. "As female adults did not have the seal applied to them for the same reason that female infants did not; and as the former have the new seal applied to them, for the same reason it should be applied to the latter also.

5. "It is to be presumed that in some of the household baptisms there were female children; but no distinction is mentioned."

---

[12] See Acts 16:14-15.

W.— "I confess that I myself did not feel the force of the objection I made, but it suggested itself to my mind, and I thought I would mention it to see how you would met it; and I am satisfied with the answer you have given. But it seems to me that in all your reasoning you proceed on the assumption that the two dispensations are, in reality, but one, with some slight, non-essential changes."

P.— "I do assume that such is the fact, and am glad of the opportunity of relieving it from the charge of being an assumption, as it is very easy to raise it to the high position of a demonstration. My proposition is that the church, from the time of its formal organization under Abraham to the end of the world, is one and the same; identical in all essential particulars. I might go back still further, but to extend the period to Abraham will suffice for our present purpose.

"The demonstration of this proposition will establish the permanence of the obligation to dedicate our children to God; for if it was a law to the church, and has not been repealed, and if the church is the same now as it was then, the inference is inevitable."

W.— "I am afraid you have undertaken a difficult task to prove, to my satisfaction, that the old Jewish Church was, in any true sense, the same as the Christian Church."

P.— "I think we will find the task very easy in the abundance of the light that the Word of God throws on it. What may be regarded as the great central necessity of the church?"

W.— "The Savior, the Lord Jesus as the God-man dying for sinners."

P.— "He is our only Savior."

W.— "Our only Savior."

P.— "Did Abraham, and David, and Isaiah, and those living under that dispensation have a Savior?"

W.— "I suppose they had."

P.— "And who was their Savior?"

W.— "There never was, nor could there be, any Savior besides Jesus."

P.— "Very good. 'Abraham,' said Jesus, 'rejoiced that he would see my day. He saw it and was glad.'[13] The Bible teaches us that there can be no salvation without a Savior; and, as you say, it teaches us that Jesus is the only Savior- not simply the only one that has been given us, but the only one that could be given us. In both dispensations, then, there was the same Savior. What is the next thing essential to salvation, or the church?"

W.— "I suppose it is the doctrine of salvation, or the manner of our being saved by the Savior."

P.— "What is the plan of salvation with us? How are we saved?"

W.— "By faith in the Lord Jesus."

P.— "And how were the Jews saved?"

W.— "The Scriptures speak of Abraham having been justified by faith."

P.— "In the fourth chapter of Romans, Paul holds up Abraham as an example to us, to show us that we are to be justified by faith. In the conclusion of the chapter, having shown that he was justified by faith, he says, 'but the words "it was counted to him" were not written for his sake alone, but for ours also. It will be counted to us who believe in him who raised from the dead Jesus our Lord.'[14] The Savior and the plan of salvation being

---

13 John 8:56.
14 Romans 4:23-24.

identical in both dispensations, what else is to be regarded as essential to the church?"

W.— "I do not think of anything that can be regarded as essential."

P.— "Nor is there anything else. The church is the body of believers, those who receive the Lord Jesus as their Savior. The mode or manner of confessing him, or making a public profession of our faith in him, may vary according to the will of God, as revealed to us. Once circumcision, by the appointment of God, was the seal of the covenant; now it is baptism by the same authority; but all the essentials are the same. The opposers of infant baptism feel the importance of building a very high wall between the two dispensations. Sometimes they seem to wish to make the impression that the gospel is peculiar to us."

W.— "I thought it was."

P.— "The gospel is the good news of salvation through Jesus. This good news came to them. Paul says, 'For good news came to us just as to them;'[15] that is, unto those living under the Old Testament dispensation. Of course, then, it was preached unto them as well as unto us. They looked forward to, and trusted in, the Savior to come. We look back to him as already come. To them he was the Lamb slain from the foundation of the world, slain in type, and slain for all the purposes of salvation.

"The apostle Paul often speaks of the identity of the church in both dispensations. In the eleventh of Romans he makes an argument of it. He represents the church as a tree, and the Jews of the old and the Gentiles of the new dispensation as branches of it— the Jews as the natural branches, and the Gentiles as taken from a wild olive tree and grafted in among them.

"Romans 11:17-21, 'But if some of the branches were broken off, and you, although a wild olive shoot, were grafted in among the

---

[15] Hebrews 4:2.

others and now share in the nourishing root of the olive tree, do not be arrogant toward the branches. If you are, remember it is not you who support the root, but the root that supports you. Then you will say, "Branches were broken off so that I might be grafted in." That is true. They were broken off because of their unbelief, but you stand fast through faith. So do not become proud, but fear. For if God did not spare the natural branches, neither will he spare you.' It is difficult to see how anyone can read such statements and fail to see that the church, under both dispensations, is one and the same.

"Paul, in writing to Timothy says, 'and how from childhood you have been acquainted with the sacred writings, which are able to make you wise for salvation through faith in Christ Jesus.'[16] When Timothy was a child there were no Scriptures but those of the Old Testament. In the next verse he says these are profitable unto all things. And in the verse quoted he declares they are able to make men wise unto salvation. By faith in Christ Jesus.

"Will you now tell me wherein I have failed to demonstrate the identity of the church under both dispensations?"

W.— "According to your view, the old Jewish church was as much entitled to be called 'Christian' as the church of the present day."

P.— "Why is it now called the Christian church?"

W.— "Because Christ is its Savior and Head."

P.— "And who was the Savior and Head of the Jewish church?"

W.— "The same Lord Jesus Christ."

P.— "Then was it not as much the Christian church as is the church under the present dispensation?"

---

[16] 2 Timothy 3:15.

W.— "I see no reason to the contrary."

P.— "Why are we called Christians?"

W.— "Because we trust in Christ."

P.— "And in whom did Abraham and his descendants trust?"

W.— "In the same Savior."

P.— "Then were they not Christians as well as we?"

W.— "For the same reason, they were."

P.— "Let us not lose sight of the question before us. In the Christian church, way back in the time of Abraham, God gave a command that Christian parents should consecrate their children to him. The law requiring it has not been fulfilled to put an end to it; it has not been repealed. Is it still binding?"

W.— "I do not see what good can be accomplished by baptizing a little child, unconscious of what is taking place."

P.— "I will leave, for the present, the question I propounded, and which you neglected to answer, and consider the difficulty you raise. What good can be accomplished by baptizing anyone?"

W.— "It is a duty imposed by Jesus."

P.— "So is the baptism of infants. But again, what good was accomplished by circumcising infants?"

W.— "But we are commanded to repent and believe, and then be baptized. Infants cannot repent nor believe, therefore they cannot be baptized."

P.— "Faith is essential to salvation. 'Whoever does not believe will be condemned.'[17] Infants cannot believe, and, therefore, they cannot be saved."

---

[17] Mark 16:16.

W.— "But that conclusion is unjustifiable, because such statements are only intended to apply to adults, or to those who can believe."

P.— "How do you know that such passages are thus restricted? I find no such restriction in the context."

W.— "There is no need to make mention of it. It is according to the very nature of things that it would be so restricted. Without so understanding such statements it would follow that all infants dying in infancy would be lost. Do you not believe they are saved?"

P.— "I believe that all such are saved."

W.— "Then you cannot believe that such passages refer to infants."

P.— "I think you have taken a correct view of such statements. My only objection is that you apply that ruled of interpretation when it suits your purpose; and when it serves a better purpose to deny it, then you deny it."

W.— "How is that?"

P.— "When repentance or faith is spoken of as a prerequisite for baptism, you find a strong argument against infant baptism, because infants cannot believe. Why do you not see that those passages which speak of faith as preceding baptism, in the very nature of the case apply only to adults who can believe?"

W.— "I acknowledge the justness of your criticism of my interpretation. The two classes of passages are similar and should be similarly interpreted. But it does seem to me unreasonable to administer baptism to an infant that knows nothing of its object or significance."

P.— "I suppose your emotions, on seeing a young child baptized, are somewhat complex: in part pity for the credulity or semi-superstition of the parents, and in part a feeling of condemnation for adding to what God has given."

W.– "I confess you have made a good analysis of my feelings when witnessing the baptism of a baby."

P.– "On the assertion that immersionists are exercised in a similar manner, it is fortunate for their comfort that they place such a small estimate on the Old Testament Scriptures, regarding them as about obsolete, and therefore devote so little attention to them."

W.– "Why so?"

P.– "Because they would become so very nervous in reading about the circumcision of little babies only eight days old. Circumcision, as we have seen, was identical with baptism in its object and significance. The very same objections can be urged against the one as against the other. But I suppose you would excuse those old Jews for such foolish practices, on account of the darkness of the period in which they lived."

W.– "But circumcision was appointed by God himself."

P.– "Exactly so. And I wish you would take the trouble to see if all the objections you urge against infant baptism could not apply with equal force against the circumcision of infants. Many silly objections are urged against infant baptism. By some it is treated with ridicule; and in the language of contempt they call it 'baby sprinkling.' But as circumcision is chargeable with precisely the same objection, of course such ridicule is directed against God himself."

W.– "One objection I have heard urged against infant baptism, and I think with some force, is the levity it produces oftentimes in the spectators. Children are generally timid and afraid of strangers. I have seen pastors whose habit it was to take the baby in their arms when baptizing it. The timidity of the child, the circumstances surrounding it, the sensation produced on it by the water, all contributing, would produce a scene bordering on the ridiculous. Now, it seems to me that a rite liable to such things does not harmonize with the solemnity that should attend an act of worship."

P.— "I am sorry that such an objection should have any weight with you. I have often heard them urged. I have seen descriptions of such scenes, given in great detail, in Baptist newspapers. In one of their Sabbath school papers, a few years ago, I saw what purported to picture of what actually occurred. The minister had the child in his arms, and was trying to baptize it, and the child was resisting with all its power, and the spectators were indulging in hearty laughter at the scene.

"To all such objections urged against the rite, it might be a sufficient answer to suggest that such scenes may not have been uncommon in connection with the circumcision of infants. To bring the matter nearer home, the same objection might be urged against the immersion of adults, as an offset to such silly charges brought against infant baptism. I know not the number of ridiculous things I have heard in connection with immersion — things so ridiculous as to render smiling on the part of the spectators excusable."

W.— "I see that such an objection should have no weight. You have made it very clear from your reference to circumcision. And I admit that similar objections might be urged against immersion. But on the assertion that the law or promise as given to Abraham was not, in any manner, repealed, is it not strange that we find no suggestion in the New Testament that it is still binding?"

P.— "Before answering that, allow me to put a question to you. On the assertion that it was to be regarded as binding, and in no sense repealed, in what way, or in what connection would you expect to find any statement setting forth such a fact?"

W.— "I would expect to find some statement affirming, or so speaking as to assume its continued obligation."

P.— "And this is just what we find in the New Testament. On the day of Pentecost, when the multitude asked, 'brothers, what shall we do?' Peter after telling them they must repent and be baptized, said, 'for the promise is for you and for your children.'[18] Peter was addressing Jews— those who were familiar with the fact that children were included in the covenant. How could they understand such language?"

W.— "I could put an interpretation upon such an expression as to avoid the force of it as an argument in favor of the continued obligation of that promise to Abraham."

P.— "I suppose that all Anti-pædobaptists do. But that is not the question. How would those who had all their lives been under a dispensation where children were included in the covenant, and had a right to the seal of that covenant, how would such understand it?"

W.— "I suppose they would look upon it as intending still to include the children."

P.— "They could put no other interpretation on it. Nor can any, if the only object is to ascertain the truth."

W.— "Are there any more such references?"

P.— "Please read 1 Corinthians 7:14."

W.— "'For the unbelieving husband is made holy because of his wife, and the unbelieving wife is made holy because of her husband. Otherwise your children would be unclean, but as it is, they are holy.'"

P.— "What does it mean?"

W.— "'Holy' is here used in the sense of legitimate."

P.— "Then suppose both parents were unbelievers, what would be the condition of their children?"

---

[18] Acts 2:37-38.

W.– "I see. It would then follow that the children of such would not be legitimate. I do not know what it means."

P.– "Its meaning is very clear. It means that, in the cases spoken of, the child would be ceremonially unclean; that is, not entitled to the seal of the covenant. It needed no explanation to the Corinthians. It is very plain to all who are willing to understand. It is one of those passages which take for granted that children have not been thrust out of the covenant."

W.– "Is it not strange, then, that among the number of baptisms recorded, no mention is made of the baptism of children?"

P.– "You must remember, that when talking on the question of mode, you found but few cases of the administration of the rite to adults. Let me ask you, on the assertion that one of our missionaries should receive into the church a husband and wife from among the heathen, and, when baptizing them, should also baptize their children, some of whom were too young to act for themselves, how would such a baptism be reported?"

W.– "He might report that he had baptized the man and his wife and their children."

P.– "Will you read Acts 16:15?"

W.– "'And after she was baptized, and her household as well...'"

P.– "Also the 33rd verse."

W.– "'And he took them the same hour of the night and washed their wounds; and he was baptized at once, he and all his family.'"

P.– "Also 1 Corinthians 1:16."

W.– "'I did baptize also the household of Stephanas. Beyond that, I do not know whether I baptized anyone else.'

"The record of these household baptisms does seem remarkable. But they may have included only those who could act for themselves. In the case of the jailer, it is stated, 'they spoke the Word of the Lord to him and to all who were in his house.'[19] This implies that his household could understand for themselves."

P.— "Does that exclude infants?"

W.— "It would if the apostles could speak to them, and they could comprehend what was spoken."

P.— "Does it imply any more than that the apostles spoke to all in his house who were capable of understanding? You must recollect that we had this question up when considering the text, 'whoever does not believe will be condemned.'[20] On the assertion that there were some in the household capable of understanding, and some who could not, would it not be proper to use the language you quote?"

W.— "I suppose it would be allowable on the principle that we are not to consider language applied to infants which, in the very nature of the case, is not applicable to them."

P.— "As a question of probabilities, are we not to conclude that there were infants in some of those households?"

W.— "I confess the probabilities are in favor of the assertion."

P.— "As we have considered the question, it stands thus: we have pointed you to a positive command, a 'Thus Says The LORD,' giving children a place in the covenant, and requiring the seal of the covenant to be applied to them. We have shown that the covenant thus made with Abraham was the covenant of grace. We have taken the position that the law so enacted as never fulfilled; could not be in its very nature; and further, it has never been repealed. Nothing short of the 'Thus Says The LORD' would be satisfactory evidence of its having been repealed. But

---

[19] Acts 16:32.
[20] Mark 16:16.

not only is it true that no such evidence can be adduced, but no passage can be pointed out from which any inference can be drawn that it was ever repealed. On the contrary, we have shown that the New Testament Scriptures award evidence, very conclusive, that it was assumed, taken for granted, that the Law was still in force. And still further, we have referred you to several household baptisms, which, taken in connection with all the other facts, renders it practically certain that baptism, the seal of the covenant under the New Testament dispensation, was applied to the infant children of believing parents. What more can you desire in the way of proof?"

W.– "You have presented the subject in a light entirely new to me. I confess it seems unanswerable. The 'positive command' and the 'Thus Says The LORD' which I required, you have furnished. I now see why you insisted on my giving the balance of the quotation from Revelation. I now see that the denial of infant baptism, and the refusal to receive it as a divine command, is taking away from what God has given us to observe. Viewed in this light, parents are certainly guilty of a great offense in neglecting to comply with the divine injunction. I can also see how sessions are culpable in quietly passing by such neglect on the part of parents."

P.– "I was certain you could not fail to see the truth when presented. As I before remarked, the unscriptural notion that immersion is baptism stands as the great obstacle in the way of all God's people seeing the truth on this subject. The two things are seen to be so incompatible that one or the other must be given up."

THE END

Scripture Index

About the Author

Dr. James McDonald Chaney was born on March 18, 1831 near Salem, Ohio. He received a Bachelors degree from William Jewell College of Missouri. A Master of Arts from King College of Tennessee, and a Doctor of Divinity from Princeton Theological Seminary were conferred to him as well.

Dr. Chaney was ordained in 1958 as a minister by the Lafayette Presbytery of the Presbyterian Church. He served regularly in several churches in Missouri, including congregations in Lamonte, Hughesville, Pleasant Hill, Corder, and Alma (all of Missouri). At the same time, Dr. Chaney served as Vice-President and then President of Elizabeth Aull Female Seminary, Lexington, Missouri. In 1885, he accepted the office of President of the Kansas City Ladies' College, and in 1891 he became President of Independence Academy of Missouri. Dr. Chaney also invented a planetarium for locating and observing celestial bodies.

In addition to *William the Baptist*, he also published *Agnes, Daughter of William the Baptist* (which was also published under the title, *The Young Theologian*).

Dr. Chaney died at his home in Independence, Missouri, on September 18, 1909.

About the Editor

Rev. John Edgar Eubanks, Jr. was born in Columbia, South Carolina, in 1972. He received a Bachelor of Arts from the University of South Carolina, and a Master of Divinity from Covenant Theological Seminary. Ordained in the Presbyterian Church in America, Rev. Eubanks serves a congregation in Eads, Tennessee.

About Doulos Resources

Our goal is to provide resources to support the church and kingdom, and to build up and encourage the pastors and leaders within the church. Our resources follow the model of Ephesians 4:12– "to prepare God's people for works of service, so that the body of Christ may be built up." We produce books, curricula, and other media resources; conduct research to advance our goals; and offer advice, counsel, and consultation. We are Reformed and Presbyterian, but not exclusively so; while we do not lay aside our theological convictions, we believe our resources may be useful across a broader theological and ecclesiastical spectrum.

Our goal with *William the Baptist*, as with all of our resources, is to offer well-edited, high-quality, and useful materials at an affordable price that makes our resources accessible to congregations and members of the church.

If you are interested in ordering additional copies of *William the Baptist*, or to order other materials that Doulos Resources offers, please visit our website: www.doulosresources.org. If you are ordering in quantity for a church or other ministry, contact us to inquire about a discount for quantity orders.

Made in the USA